PWA

OSCAR MOORE was born in 1960 and grew up in London. Educated at Haberdashers' Aske's Boys' School, Elstree, and Pembroke College, Cambridge, he worked as a journalist, contributing to *Time Out*, *Punch*, *i-D*, *The Times*, the *Mail on Sunday*, the *Evening Standard*, and the *Fred*. He was appointed editor of *Screen International* in 1990 and later became its editor-in-chief. His novel *A Matter of Life and Sex* was originally published under the pseudonym Alec F. Moran and is published under his real name by Penguin. Oscar Moore died on 12 September 1996.

OSCAR MOORE

PWA

LOOKING AIDS IN THE FACE

PICADOR

First published 1996 by Picador

an imprint of Macmillan Publishers Ltd
25 Eccleston Place, London SW1W 9NF
and Basingstoke

Associated companies throughout the world

ISBN 0 330 35193 1

1 3 5 7 9 8 6 4 2

A CIP catalogue record for this book is available from the British Library

Typeset by CentraCet Limited, Cambridge
Printed by Mackays of Chatham plc, Chatham, Kent

PWA

Oscar Moore
823 Palms Blvd.
Venice
California
90291 USA

1st March 1994

Jodie Tresidder
188 Spring Road
Huntington
New York
11743 USA

Dear Jodie,

Well, maybe this sunshine and salsa cure is working. After a rough start which last night had me hitting the fast-acting downers (Sevredol – pink and pernicious) to kill a foghorn-meets-lighthouse headache, this morning I have survived the brightness of the sun, the gloppiness of a plate of oatmeal and apple (guaranteed to make you poop, it said on the menu), the stickiness of French toast with blueberry butter and the heavenliness of a Fruit Fuck, a kind of kiwi-green punch packed with the sort of seafaring algae that whales eat (well, I am trying to put some weight back on). I have even had exercise – I cycled down flat streets in bright sun to the restaurant where this ozone-friendly breakfast was wolfed on a sun-splashed patio while reading tales of Glaswegian criminal horror in the latest *Granta*.

You may not believe this but this is a breakthrough. Cycling! And yesterday I went with Bart (instant CV: Bart Everly, 35, freelance photographer and retired dope fiend, gay, good-looking in that hayseed kind of a way that comes from being born in South Bend, Indiana, long-standing friend and co-doper, my host at his rented architect-designed CalipostMexmodern Venice house-and-garden) to the Marina Athletic Club and swam ten lengths in the outdoor pool despite a wind-chill factor that dropped the temperature from 70 or so to 60 or less. Now admittedly my normal routine is forty lengths (and a couple of circuits of Greater London) and my juvenile cycling career became a legend (not least because it engendered an entire sexual career later summarized in a brief little memoir entitled *A Matter of Life and Sex*) but you are listening to a man who for the last two months has only winced and blanched at the mention of physical exertion, who found that years of addiction to swimming pools (it's the water not the nudity, honest) had faded to a fear of mid-length drowning (not very fashionable this season) and who looked at a bicycle as if at some intriguing rack on which to stretch young children.

I have, I will admit, managed to get my early morning press-ups back to forty, but my sit-ups, arm-curls, shoulder-extensions and hair-pieces are a thing of the past (I tried some sit-ups about a month ago and spent the rest of the day bent double, which is especially awkward when trying to eat without dribbling and pee without . . . well . . . dribbling).

So I am in a VERY GOOD MOOD. But the main reason

that I am in this VERY GOOD MOOD is because the foghorn/lighthouse has 'stopped' (I put this in inverted commas because it has only been two hours of painlessness and I do not want to tempt fate). My stomach disorder is largely under control. I wince and blanch, of course, but don't we all and if we don't we should. I have problems with sudden bends and major pressures (I could not have done any more than ten lengths yesterday without giving birth) and although my plate of oatmeal promised instant poops I have an on-off affair with morphine-induced constipation. But these headaches were getting to be very depressing, disconcerting and even despairing. They were not continuous, just flashing and blaring in thirty-second intervals, but they felt like pressure pumps building from my bowels and exploding above my left eye (on the way rendering my arms useless and leaving a residue of pain in every left-side molar). They had me howling like a child and last night they had me doped up and whimpering. They have been happening for five days and yesterday panic began to set in after advil, anadin, paracetamol, tylenol, aspirin, Sevredol and meditation had failed to even briefly divert the pain. So I called my sister back in Bishop Auckland and checked that it wasn't meningitis, but apparently that comes with a stiff neck and over-sensitive eyes (I think of my eyes as highly, but not over-sensitive). Anyway today (Tuesday) was going to be take-the-bull-by-the-horns-day, and I was going to throw caution (approximately $100) to the wind and call a doctor who could then stare into my eyes and tell me what was wrong. Now I am sitting here with everything from my eyes to my legs crossed and the $100 still in my pocket hoping that I have gotten away with it.

I should tell you that the last time a doctor stared in my eyes he told me that I had lacerations of the small intestine and a twisted gut. Normally people comment on how blue or intelligent or, depending on the time of day and the number of Jamaican cigarettes burnt, how red and small or, depending on the number of Sevredol swallowed, how pinned my eyes are. Now, if someone did that to you, looked deep into your azures and whispered, 'I can see lesions in your gut,' you might be a little put off and tell them where to get off. I, however, very nearly fell on the neck of this Dr Hansard, and immediately signed up for eighteen months of thrice-weekly sessions at a knockdown price of £20 a session and swallowed several teaspoons of a thick crimson herbal brew called Dragon's Blood. My credulousness only began to waver when he suddenly said to me apropos of nothing, 'It's OK to cry you know, Oscar.' I instantly teared up and would have begun to bucket had the nutritionist not been standing behind Dr Hansard. I just didn't feel like a performing Pavlovian right then and resisted. I later repeated this little manoeuvre to another former patient of said Hansard (who had been told he was hypoglycaemic on the basis of little more than a handshake) and he tutted as he remembered the same little game being played with him.

Dr Hansard is not a mainstream doctor (hence the £20 a session and the Dragon's Blood), but rather a practitioner of Tibetan-Bon medicine, which from his perspective is clearly a Bon idea, because it involves almost no direct treatment and a lot of vague, 'Do you feel better after lying down in that dark room for half an hour while we simply went on with our business?' treatment. I tell you, the last three visits have involved nothing more than me lying down and having a burning herbal stick (a.k.a. a Moxa) passed up and down my body, only inches from my skin. Soothing, yes. But as it happens I have my own Moxa at home and don't quite understand why I should spend an hour on the Tube and £60 a week having someone else do it to me. But like most of Dr Hansard's patients, I was desperate for something.

I went to him first at the beginning of February, a month into the stomach saga, but I shall not be going back when I get back from my LA health drive. What began to undermine my enthusiasm for this huggy-smiley-warmy-sicky medicine and Dr Hansard himself were the certificates on the surgery wall from the International Open University of Complementary Medicines in Colombo. Even on my first visit these two trophies begged questions. The first was elementary geopolitics. Where the fuck is Colombo? I knew I knew or had known once. I knew too he had been a TV detective. But it wasn't until I picked up that week's *Time Out* and read a follow-up piece by Duncan Campbell to his own television documentary on undercover AIDS cures and how unfortunate young men like me were being ripped off by unscrupulous quacks peddling crystalline urine and blood mixes under bogus health cure labels that it came home. All the 'doctors' featured in the programme and mentioned in the article had received their 'degrees' from the IOUCM, which Campbell described as a private back-street acupuncture clinic in a suburb of the Sri Lankan capital. Now Colombo is not famous as the source of medical wisdom or honourable academics. Indeed, this little clinic has been dispensing more than degrees; it has conferred professorships and knighthoods with a blithe contempt for protocol, and the head of the clinic is the self-styled His Lordship Doctor Professor Sir someone Jayasekera.

You can imagine that this made me feel vulnerable, hurt, cheated, angry and determined to confront medicrime on site. Well, yes, everything but the latter. I went back (only three more times) and submitted to more Moxa, but all the time I wasn't really submitting, I was investigating, until finally, last Friday I said loudly to myself, 'This is the last time you come here.' Actually I was already out of the door by then so I don't think that counts as brave confrontation, but you see I was really thinking about the other patients. I couldn't face the idea of shattering their illusions. The clinic was full of poor defenceless Kensington dowagers and misled young men with long hair and fashionable boots. Some of the women wept into their cashmere and pearls as they arrived, wracked by fears of potential illnesses lurking in the air, and some of the young men looked in urgent need of a new mantra. Who was I to disrupt their hard-won security, to deny their faith in ginger and cinnamon tea, to undermine their belief in small manipulations of minor muscles in return for major banknotes? Not I. I had other battles to fight. I have my inner demons to contend with.

My inner demons made a smart move settling in my stomach. I cannot think of another place where they could have guaranteed themselves more attention. The stomach (which in my case is just a nice word for bowel, so maybe we should settle for guts) is the fulcrum of every tension, hope, fear and anticipation. It is the repository of all input and the processor of all output. It – or they – can turn my face white, my mouth dry and my jaw loose with just one squeeze of pain. And the pain. THE PAIN.

I am not in much pain any more, in fact. In the last day since starting this letter my foghorn-lighthouse appears to have exhausted itself, which is a tremendous liberation. But I am suffering from a condition I have christened 'residual panic'. This is an early (probably tribal) pain memory, which, activated by the merest jellybelly twinge, the smallest griping of a raw stomach lining, grips my diaphragm and squeezes it, punctures my lungs and seizes my throat until my breathing resembles that of a marathon runner with asthma. This breathing disorder triggers its own pain which then worsens the breathing disorder, locking me in a dizzying spiral of disability.

Of course, the pain memory does not have to go very far back. Less than a month ago I was writhing on my sofa, clinging to a midday joint, howling for morphine and generally playing patient-terrible. Two months ago – and that is where the story really starts – I was chewing cushions, carpets and other people's fingernails, jack-knifed on the hearth in front of a dimming fire as all around me friends and friends of friends gallivanted on E, seeing in the New Year with narcotic exuberance.

But first a flash-forward to life in LA where the temperature daily soars into the eighties and the sun is too hot to sit in unless you go to windy beaches off Malibu (where the debris from broken homes – bits of storm-shattered building, not wayward children – sprawls down the collapsed cliffs towards the tiny strips of sand).

Fenton and Randy came by to grab some pasta supper before leaving for New York and snowstorms. They have a day of meetings today all of which are probably cancelled because of the snow making it impossible for high-level honchos (who always live out of town) to get into work, and then are coming back so I hope to see a lot more of them at the weekend. Apparently they had great fun with Sam and Josh. Please inform me of anybody else you plan to introduce my godson to in advance of such meetings. I must have his moral fibre at heart. And these two are dangerous iconoclasts, capable of insane attacks on the supposedly plummeting living standards in London and general slandering of everything British (and honourable) from taxis to telephones. I'm not sure why, but I seem to have this fierce loyalty to London and sort of partially by extension a weaker loyalty towards England. This was tried and tested on a daily basis by Patrick (Do you remember Patrick? He is now a notorious television chef in Holland, who has hurtled to celebrity by stuffing mice and serving their brains in aspic at a dinner party which landed him on radio, television and in court in that order), who used to deride the British as the retards of Europe. Instead of siding with my Dutch relatives I always found myself muttering bitterly, 'Well in that case what are you doing here, if it is really so awful?'

Anyway tempers almost frayed (I mean my temper almost snapped) when this airy ex-pat Liverpudlian queen called Paul Fortune – apparently, and *he* said this which makes it rather worthless because you should never trumpet your own CV at the table (I mean I didn't even tell him what I did for a living ... come to think of it, he never asked), voted one of the top ten interior designers in America in 1987 (which immediately prompts the question, 'Well, honey, where have you been since then?') – joined in the attack with his disdainful fag voice. He was one of these people that puts up a red rag to my bull, and hell can I be bullish. You know, one of those people who thinks he knows the final word on everything from magazines to MTV and sneers at disagreement with an affectedly tired disdain. In fact, a person just like me, which is why I argued with him, ingratiated myself with him, name-dropped at him, prostituted my ego before his scrawny self-importance and then badmouthed him as soon as he was out of the door. One typical exchange: I told him I had been asked if I would be interested in writing Derek Jarman's biography (which I have – by Jonathan Burnham at Chatto – and am CONSIDERING, but only if I quit *Screen*, which I may have to do if this illness proves too resilient and too susceptible to stress because *Screen* is like stress-concentrate) and he immediately said that I should interview him. SO COOL AND SCEPTICAL TO THE LAST, I immediately said how that was what everyone immediately said and he immediately got a little bit huffy and said how he knew Derek *really* well, and I of course said that that too was what everybody said, and gave him a cool get-out by telling him that in most cases it was true. Anyway, he made my skin crawl and yet I crawled as he left by saying I'd be on the phone as soon as the deal was done (which given the amount of money I am sure that Chatto will put up, may never be. I mean, honey, I have a lifestyle to support, even in sickness I need wealth, and there is no way that my entourage can be fed and clothed on less than $30,000).

Flash-forward two: Dinner with Barnaby and Christina yesterday and Barnaby assures me that the headaches, which have now returned rolling in along with the ocean fog and a chill wind, are all part of the same shingle problem. That pleased me. I shall simply triple my dose of Zovirax and treat myself to extra morphine tonight because of all the stress I have been under thinking I was ill with something new.

Saw *Reality Bites* and felt like somebody's parent trying to find their kids in a nightclub. Twenty-three doesn't seem that long ago, but I fell right into the generation gap on this movie. Of course it is 'very MTV', which along with 'he's in denial' seems to be phrase of the Zeitgeist. But actually, once you get past all the mixed-media video footage and narcissistic self-obsession, it is just a love story between the beast man and the beauty girl. Ethan Hawke is an OK beast man but he is too beastly to ever be charming and you find yourself secretly praying for Brad Pitt (but in fact all and any of these smart-arsed post-student types with their volleys of bitter and twisted 'wisdom' falling like shrapnel on intimidated oiks, and their 'I'm too clever to get off my butt' posturing, are just too painful (and painfully recognizable) to be taken seriously. I'll take my wit from wiser men, if you please. The posy world-WEARINESS of boys and girls who have yet to face the real world in a real embrace (i.e., not MTV, movies, comics, etc.) is tired and tedious). Winona is cool but seems like she's on day release from being a movie star and this is just such fun she can do it without thinking too much. After all, everything's cool as long as you have a cigarette in your mouth.

I'm ten years older than these people. I could be their father's lover. Maybe I should be taking them under my wing. Anyway it was interesting voyeurism into the popcornheads of a half-generation hence and it cheered me up because I'd had a lousy day of aches and pains and needed a little escapism.

It's weird how the film gets off on cigarettes too. Everyone is smoking and lighting cigarettes and talking about cigarettes, even quoting them in the movie-within-the-movie (thankfully they are Camels so at least I am smoking a strategic brand – maybe I'm an undercover agent from the parental police). And the other night at dinner everybody was smoking. Humph. Could this be a magazine article or an episode of *The Late Show*: the collapse of health culture, the return to nicotine. And then do an extended item on rising levels of unsafe sex among pre-consent juveniles and then link that back to the single-parent family and too much child support. It could be a political platform.

Anyway, to return to the illness saga, everything fell apart at New Year. Nothing like starting as you mean to go on!

The above incriminated friends were a bunch of ten of us who had invaded Mary Arnold-Forster's grandmother's Gothic-revival mansion on the Mull of Kintyre for five days of drinking and walking and drugs and big dinners. So you may say I deserve everything I got and for a while I thought so too, especially as the first pangs on New Year's Eve came immediately after a line of cocaine which I had vowed to never take again (after the fourth line the night before). But then the pain grew and swelled and expanded and began to eat me alive. This was big hurt.

By Monday I was too sick to walk or talk and was bundled into the back of our Nissan Micra. (Useful tip when renting cars – avoid anything with the word micra, micro, mini, or magic. These cars are always about six inches long and have enough leg room for a legless insect in the back.) Anyway I was squashed in, ankles somewhere round my neck (but no pleasure anticipated) as we hurtled (and very nearly hurled) through the rain round the crags and cliffs of a spectacularly grim coastline to Campbeltown. The doctor at the little hospital there (the same doctor who had examined me earlier and suggesting I had bad wind had given me some pink gunge to make me belch) decided things were getting serious (he was a very wise man) and arranged for an ambulance to collect me from the tarmac at Glasgow airport (I had a plane ticket for the ten-seater from Campbeltown that afternoon). By this stage I was past caring where I ended up and was facing up to the fact that I wasn't going to be back at the office the next morning as expected. Now countless mornings later I am still not back at my beloved desk working my beloved ass off and feeling, at least for a few hours a day, at the centre of the universe (well, the universe of weekly film trades).

But my gratitude at the willingness of Glasgow to admit me, my pleasure at being stretchered and lifted into an ambulance by solicitous ambulance men and my delight at being given my first jab of Pethidine and subsiding into a distant world of smiles and soft edges was short-lived because here commenced five days of purgatory in a twenty-three-bed prison ward in Glasgow Southern General, during which I didn't sleep, I didn't shit, I just lived, prostrate and moaning from Pethidine jab to Pethidine jab. Each jab gave me grinning satisfaction for two hours but I was only allowed one jab every four hours and by the time the four hours were up a new sister would be on the ward who didn't believe I was authorized to have any Pethidine until every other painkiller (weaker or totally ineffective) had been tried on me, so then there followed two hours of angry debate until finally they relented

. . . and Oscar had won another two hours of respite. Even the Pethidine began to fade after a while as my butt developed the texture of a dartboard and my skin felt like heat-dried flaky pastry and seemed to be flaking off in front of me, grated by heavily starched sheets until I was screaming for Calamine Lotion like a kid with chickenpox . . . hah, prescient, as we shall see.

I had some tests – on the Wednesday – and the (negative) results came through on the Friday. The rest was just hanging around watching TV, reading *The Sun*, and trying to sleep through a nagging, gnawing internal calamity. They ruled out kidney stones and a few other emergency extremes and then they seemed to lose interest in me. It may be incipient paranoia but I was sure I detected hostility among some of the nurses, who after all knew I was English (bad news in a Glasgow hospital), HIV and gay (at least I presume they did because it was written down on my paperwork as I was checked in), and Scottish nurses, angelic though they sometimes may be, are not known for their political wisdom or the breadth of their sexual tolerance. As someone pointed out to me later, it is not by accident that so many of them marry policemen.

There was open hostility between me and at least one nurse and two sisters, but that seemed to be the case for the rest of the ward too, including Jamie on one side of me, who had been stabbed in the lung and carried a plastic flask with him all the time half full of pink gunge that leaked down a tube from a hole in his back, and the old man next to me who had to be told – in strict, clipped Glaswegian with no glimmer of warmth – that his leg would have to go above the knee.

But by the end of the week I was convinced the doctors

were sick of the sight of me too. Which is hard to credit when you think how little they saw of me or me of them. They would come by in a little posse of white coats, all different ages, some students, one carrying a little baton as if each patient were a drawing on the anatomy blackboard, and they would crawl up the ward. They moved so slowly, whole days seemed to come and go before they reached my bed, by which time I was transfixed, mouth open, ready for the verdict, a decision, a diagnosis, some action. But instead they would mumble briefly to each other about the fact that they still had not seen the results from the tests two days earlier and therefore nothing more could be said or tried at this stage and anyway they had been on the phone with my doctor at the Middlesex Hospital who had said they would be happy to have me . . . so in other words fuck off. So I did.

Friday afternoon, dosed up to my eyeballs in codeine, I took a cab to the airport and by lying down every ten minutes and using my luggage trolley as a Zimmer frame I got on a flight back to London without anyone at British Midland noticing that my natural posture was doubled up and my welcoming warm smile was actually a sweaty grimace of pain.

Throughout this illness I have been giving myself deadlines for recovery (deadlines immediately after which I am going to work, going to a party, hosting a dinner for eight people) which I then reach and break and re-set (I did go back to work, for a week, and left iller than I was when I went in; I did host a dinner for eight people and the sight of the washing-up almost carved me in two, it sent such lightning rods of pain to my stomach). The first deadline was this first weekend in January, when I decided that instead of checking myself straight into the Middlesex I would sit it out at home over the weekend, because I might even be better by Monday and then I could avoid all the bother and trouble of checking into a whole new hospital. Big joke. I had to learn the slow and painful way. By Saturday morning I was screaming for assistance. That was one of the worst nights to date, throwing back the codeine and smoking joints, huddled under duvets on the sofa watching anything that passed down the television tube in an effort to keep some of my mind off a pain that came in great wavelike contractions. When I was out of it enough I felt as if I was surfing on muscle contractions. That aspect of this whole saga has at least changed now. The pain when it is there is more like stiff muscles and the exhaustion of jellybelly. (I am currently wracked by a diarrhoea that wakes me up in the morning and by 9 a.m. has left me with a hollow yearning in my belly which I always interpret as hunger until food hits the hypersensitive lining of my rattled stomach and sends me into a two-hour gut spasm – but isn't that what holidays are all about, getting to know your bowels?) No longer, thanks to the great god Zovirax, these endless labour-like pulses that left me tossing like an abandoned dinghy on stormy waves. Now it is simple, even wincing and the occasional 'I had better lie down for a few minutes'. I feel like a soldier with old war wounds that tend to play up when washing up, cleaning and any other form of disagreeable exertion are suggested. I do make a very good front-seat car passenger however, and am happy to be left in the car while the driver runs errands. I cherish my moments of peace and quiet parked on the side of a busy street listening to the radio and daydreaming about Saturday morning shopping expeditions with my dad as a kid when he was always nipping in and out of electrical hardware shops while we fooled around with the radio and pretended to drive (until someone hit the hooter and we were told to get back into our seats). See the world. Just don't engage with it.

Anyway, come Saturday morning I was on the phone to the Middlesex pleading for a bed (and I must say they were incredibly efficient and welcoming, with the chief consultant ringing me at home from his home to assure me everything would be ready for me) and then painfully inched my way to the hospital and fell back waiting for the healing hands. Suddenly I was in paradise. This was like a four-star hotel, where they are pleased to see you and serve you. For a start it was an HIV ward, so there was no unpleasant undertone. (Of course there was a rather unpleasant overtone – this was, after all my first stay in a full-fledged HIV ward, and I recognized some of the emaciated faces coughing up bilious phlegm in private rooms from bars and clubs of the last ten or twenty years . . . but at this time I was in too much pain to care, I just wanted relief.) The whole atmosphere after the stiff starched white uniforms and Aryan politics of Glasgow was like sinking into the deep sofa of a hotel lobby and being plied with cakes. (Oh, and that was another thing about Glasgow – even if I had been able to eat, the food on offer was of such tiny portions that I would have been racked by hunger. I have lost over a stone in the past two months. I stare at old photos of myself and see whole areas of body that no longer exist.)

The nurses were in jeans and T-shirts and were intelligent and funny, the doctors came round several times a day to try different tests, nobody argued about my supplies of morphine and in the end they plugged a pump into my belly that kept me happy and quiet for the rest of my stay. As soon as they spotted the chickenpox craters on my arms and legs they moved me into my own room where I was visited almost all day and spent happy evenings sitting watching television and smoking spliffs with Jon Spiteri, occasionally interrupted by spasms, drips, pump changes and blood-pressure readings. The nurses seemed blithely unconcerned that I was smoking weed in my little one-man ward, and I found that the joints hit the morphine and combined in a wibbly-wobbly high that left me beached on a bank of pillows, grinning inanely at the TV. Now, out in the cruel real world with all its hard edges and physical demands, that period seems like a dopey nirvana. I sometimes have hankerings to be picked up and sent straight back to my little room. But of course all the time I was in there I was planning my check-out date, moving it forwards day by day.

The big turning point came at the hands of a masseur. The pain of the muscle contractions had by now become inextricably intertwined with the pain of massive constipation. Health is not for the squeamish, is it? But then anyone who has had children has I hope long since lost their anal innocence. So forgive my inch by inch calibration of each and every bowel change, movement and blockage. These things are now of paramount importance in my life. I live by the uneven rhythm of my guts. Anyway, by the second day in my private suite I was screaming for enemas. I had not felt a single flicker of peristalsis for two weeks and was so perpetually whacked out on opiates that none seemed likely. Plus I was eating very little, so there was little incentive for my insides to deal with anything. But the pain was approximating my imagined version of childbirth. My belly bloated as if someone had stuck a balloon pump in my navel and worked it. I lay and groaned and groaned and lay and every time I saw a nurse I asked if we could try another enema. I just needed relief. I dreamt of being emptied. But they can only give you so many enemas a day and they were scared to give me the most severe laxative (something called Go Lightly which they claimed could bore through concrete) because there was so little in my stomach anyway and forcibly evacuating it like that might leave my muscles in painful fluttering spasm – exactly the colitis we were trying to cure.

Then one of the nurses told me that a masseur was in the ward who had had some success in relieving constipation and she thought he should work on me. This man was a genius. I lay there, my poor wracked belly upturned and naked and he just stroked it, a few strokes this way, a few that, a couple of circular motions. His hands were like feathers brushing the air over my stomach. He was only there for ten minutes but immediately he started I felt seismic shifts in my innards. Noises, creaks, strange inner churnings. I just lay there. I swear, the whole night I did not change position. I just listened to the movements, like crocodiles sliding through the swamp, and watched television and smiled because for the first time in two weeks I felt as if something was happening. It happened the next day at midday. Oscar slipped out of bed clutching his pump and gave birth. It would be unbecoming to describe what I achieved, produced, what emerged from this wracked body, but suffice it to say afterwards I lay there and felt the aftershocks shaking my limp and empty body and I smiled some more because I felt like the champion long-distance runner, racked with pain but knowing he has won the race. Nurses put their heads round the door to congratulate me (news this big travels fast) and friends who came to visit were treated to smiles and tentative attempts to approximate the enormity of my achievement.

From there it seemed a mere formality, waiting for my exeat. I sat out the weekend cosy and comfortable with the newspapers, books, visitors and little trips into the outside world. Actually, the first of these was rather a rude shock. I could not walk. I could walk but no faster than an infirm ninety-year-old. I felt as light and fragile as a piece of cracked Meissen. I crept, one foot gingerly placed after the other, down Charlotte Street but was almost swept away in the rip tides of Oxford Street. I suddenly felt totally helpless, knowing that if one person walked into me I was finished. I would probably sprawl back into another who would push me away and I would be bounced between hostile bodies until I fell. I crept along, clinging to the wall, emaciated, etiolated, wrapped up in jackets and scarves and hat, and feeling very conspicuously a PWA (Person With Aids). I used to work in Charlotte Street and I used to see them walking down the street on brief release from hospital, that peculiar gaunt grimace eating away at their faces, the unshaven chin, the pallor, the tremble in the arm even as it worked the walking stick(s). I have seen them and like everyone else felt the shadow of death cross my path. And here I was sitting in Pret à Manger, staring at the world with a sort of panicked fascination, pacing my muesli and yoghurt and fruit juice, terrified of the prospect of struggling back to the hospital, feeling and looking like these nightmare wraiths.

Thankfully I had pre-rolled a joint, so I stopped in Newman Street, leaned back against the wall and smoked before inching my way back to the hospital where I spent the next thirty minutes sitting in the well-stuffed easy chairs in the lobby watching the to and fro of patients.

A young man arrived in an ambulance and was wheeled in on a high-standing bed. He had a plaster on the left-hand side of his forehead and was in pyjamas. From the expression on his face I knew immediately that he was checking in to my ward or the sister AIDS ward next door. There was something about the resignation, the residue of bitterness and the quiet lonely bravery all readable in his face that summed up so much of our (gay male) experience of AIDS. When so many have died you cannot exaggerate your own chances. When you have seen so many die you recognize the first signs and the shaky defences of your own optimism. It is grappling with the inexorable that makes this such hard work. And knowing that you are turning from a person into a casualty. That was the dreadful gloom that sank into my head while reading Randy Shilts' *And The Band Played On*. That everybody gay seemed to be dead or dying or seriously bereaved by the end of the book. And now, I read today that Randy Shilts himself has died. Derek too. And the list stretches back into distant memory now. But it is an honourable roll-call.

What I had forgotten, as I sat grinning and content in my little room, interrupted only by telephone calls and deliveries of flowers (and, as the day wore on, visitors) was that I was completely buoyed on morphine, leaking directly into my bloodstream twenty-four hours a day.

That was the rude shock when I left the hospital and the

pump was dismantled and replaced with pills. Pills do not go directly into your bloodstream. Large amounts can go unabsorbed, in fact. Having been anticipating a triumphant return home, I was instead laid low (on the sofa under the duvet in front of the television – how low can you go?). The cocktail party for an old schoolteacher that I had promised to attend came and went as I lay on my bed and groaned, incapable of even standing up to get changed, my planned return to work (on Monday, on Wednesday, on Friday, on next Monday . . .) came and went, people came and went and I was all the time howling and groaning and buckling up with pain. So they doubled my dose of morphine sulphate, and doubled it again, and gave me additional fast-acting morphine (the pink and pernicious) which friends ate greedily and then felt queasy for days and began to forswear downers in public as if the whole experience had regurgitated unwelcome memories. And then finally I was comfortable and could concentrate on eating and growing and getting better.

It has to be said that I feel a great deal better now and have regained a large chunk of the lost weight. It has to be said too that my stomach still hurts quite a lot of the time and feels as if it always will. And maybe as bad is the nervous anticipation of pain even when it is not hurting. I am learning to live with this but my reluctance is expressed in anxiety. And I am wrestling with some ancient demons, demons who have been hovering on the horizon for a year or so and which I have turned away from each time, blindly burying myself in the very work, devoting myself to the very same frenetic social and professional gallop that they were chuckling about all along: Why do you work so hard, is it to find yourself or to avoid looking for yourself? Why are you such a victim of your own Protestant work ethic that you cannot even sit on the sofa with a book without wondering whether you shouldn't be doing something more active, less pleasurable, but easily defined as work? Why is your sense of self and self-esteem so bound up with your work? Why do you not believe that people like you, when they make it so clear that they do, and why are you so panicked by the fact that people may not like you; do you have an opinion of yourself you are refusing to face up to? Why can't you be well when everybody else is, except the people who aren't and they don't count which is what is driving you mad, because you are beginning to decide that you don't count now? Is suicide laziness, cowardice, cynicism or rebellion?

While initially it may be comforting to blame things on stress rather than HIV, the fact is, as we have already said, that the two are inextricably intertwined, along with age and the accumulative effect of all three. I have felt very fragile, mentally, for the past few months. I had my first stress attack in the summer when I went away for a month to the Midwest to write and suffered the most appalling attack of haemorrhoids ever (and this on a trip when I was making ten-hour drives). They were finally operated on in November. I have had KS on my arms and legs and it has spread throughout the year. I have itchy spots and itchy rashes on my face and back and chest and arms. These two have been going on for a while. I have not felt as if I am in control of what is going on for as long as these problems have been active.

I know each and everybody has their hidden pain. I have been lucky throughout my youth and life. I was never sick.

Now that I have no physical defences I find myself with very few mental defences.

I think a lot about death. Not dying, which I may still be 'in denial' about. But death, sudden, swift, final and decorated with memorial services and obituaries. I feel left out, left behind, marginalized, when in fact I was driving myself insane with an overwhelming schedule. Was this already a deathwish? Am I really that scared that the second novel will be a disappointment (and does it really matter that much if it is?).

But all is not lost. I am having a good time. I am justifying work breaks and then enforcing them by smoking joints. I am being entertained by (and maybe entertaining) old friends. I am seeing films. My appetite for food and for life are back. So what if there is a residue of pain? Maybe that will be enough to place new limits on my own self-destructive work drive and remind me to live each day carefully because there may not be enough left to go round.

It's weird. Sometimes it makes me want to cry and sometimes, not often, I actually manage to. It makes me look at the world more keenly and yet sometimes I feel as if I am looking at it through someone else's window.

I am going to post this now. I look forward to hearing from you and give my love to Pud and the boys.

Lots of love

OSCAR

This is where it all started: writing this letter cracked the problem for me. Now I knew I could write about being ill and make it somehow simultaneously funny, cathartic and therapeutic. Now all I had to do was recover, get home and ring *The Guardian*.

I had bumped into *The Guardian*'s Deborah Orr at the French House Dining Room a month or so before Christmas 1993 and she had asked me if I would be interested in writing occasional pieces for the Weekend section, which she was editing (and still is).

We had worked together at Forward Publishing, where I had been editor of *The Edge*, a quarterly publication for Thames Television, and she was the startlingly irascible and quite brilliant sub.

I'm not just saying this to guarantee more work. Any journalist knows the value of a great sub-editor, who can trim the excess from an article and leave no scars (the journalistic equivalent of cosmetic surgery). A great sub makes you look good and certainly better than you deserve, and therefore is a friend and ally to be respected, cultivated . . . and concealed to avoid any embarrassing public revelations (like how much of that last piece was actually written by you or how much had to be cut despite a very specific brief that asked for 1,200 words and not the 2,000 you eventually provided a week after deadline).

In the time since we had last worked together I had also published a book, *A Matter of Life and Sex*, an autobiography thinly disguised as a novel, which Deborah had read and apparently enjoyed.

I was very flattered and very interested in her suggestion, but felt that if this was going to develop into more than the occasional contribution written in haste in the non-existent spare time from my main job as editor of the film trade weekly *Screen International*, it would have to have some guiding theme.

Little did I suspect that such a theme was just about to present itself.

I say that I little suspected the disaster that befell me that New Year's Eve in Scotland, but I had been heading for a medical catastrophe for some time, and recent strange skin trouble, oral thrush and a series of major stress attacks at work, coupled with a cross-Channel relationship that seemed in danger of sinking midstream, were on the verge of bringing everything to a head.

In fact my life was about to implode and that curious determination to keep the mind and body in self-contained, airtight compartments was about to be made to look ridiculous. Mine was a system on the verge of collapse, waiting for a decisive event to convert all the gathering symptoms of ARC into a full-fledged AIDS diagnosis.

The trigger was a panic-stricken stress attack in November 1993 (see letter) but the impact was not felt until New Year's Eve.

AIDS has always been a disease of delayed reactions (or at least had been, but recently isolated mutant strains appear to be devastatingly lethal and fast, with victims succumbing in a matter of months after 'conversion'). I believe I was 'converted' to HIV-positive in the summer of 1983, while misbehaving in New York (definitely a case of the wrong place at the wrong time). I cannot be sure, as I did not get tested until 1987, but memories of one bathhouse night (among many) stick in my mind as the culprit.

I was playing tag on the Village front line and got hit and hurt. That was in the earliest days of the virus, when it still did not have a name, but had won the media nickname 'gay cancer'. A ten-year 'incubation' period followed, during which the body successfully resisted the depredations of the virus. This was not uncommon. (All the same it is strange to realize that all my professional working life has been lived under the shadow of the virus. But by the time the shingles hit, I had known something was going to give in/up/out sooner rather than later.)

There were a couple of other key inspirations for the column; basically reading other writers including Harold Brodkey in *The New Yorker*, writing about being sick and reading about the runaway success of a book written by another journalist, called *My Breast* and dealing with her having been diagnosed as suffering from breast cancer. I didn't buy this latter book, but when I read (avidly) another *New Yorker* piece, written (beautifully) by an elderly contributor and describing in gripping (and by now familiar) detail the landscape and political/emotional climate of a world of waiting rooms, delayed appointments and the unwelcome camaraderie of the sick, I felt myself warming to a theme. The letter to Jodie only clinched it.

I believed that there was an audience out there, of the sick, of relatives and carers of the sick, and even of well people with no immediate threat to their well-being, who nevertheless liked having their curiosity (about life on the other side of the sick/well looking-glass) satisfied. It seems I was right; whether I was tapping into an eternal truth or just switching on to the Zeitgeist by iterating and therefore massaging people's eternal health anxieties, my lively and often terribly moving mailbag was the most concrete evidence that I, speaking from my demographically narrow PWA platform, was nonetheless reaching a very broad church. Some were the people I would have hoped and expected to reach: frightened teenagers who had not yet come out to their parents, the lovers and friends and parents of AIDS victims – some already deceased – and occasionally an AIDS victim him(principally)self.

But perhaps the most moving – and indeed the largest part – of my correspondence came from the disinterested, but manifestly not uninterested, compassionate onlookers from Cornwall to Inverness-shire. It was an extraordinary experience – reading through a week's haul of mail and feeling at once moved, cheered and awed by the breadth (social, geographical, in age and in belief) of my audience. Writing can be a very isolated life: sitting alone at the desk in the corner of my bedroom with my back to the window and the yells of the street-market below, the rest of the world dissolves out of sight (especially today, when I would have trouble seeing them if they stood in front of me and waved a red flag). Illness, too, can be very isolating. Although I have a handful of very devoted friends, there are many others who have faded out of sight (not the fault of my fading sight this time), understandably dissolving into the hinterland (for them the upfront, immediate and real) of their own lives.

I feel sometimes as if I have been keeping up a one-sided but nonetheless profoundly satisfying correspondence with all these absent friends, and then when I meet them (at a wedding, birthday party or just by accidental street collision – always a hazard for the very partially sighted) I find that the letters have indeed got through and they are incredibly up to date on my condition, and ready with those soothing and well-targeted sympathies.

This may all sound very selfish. Maybe I should be using my column to badger and heckle the powers that be, but the truth is that so far they have been treating me very well – the occasional cutback notwithstanding – and I am better at articulating my own daily travails than seizing, and waving, someone else's banner. This column has become a lifeline: I can use it to hector and embarrass recalcitrant politicians, pharmaceutical companies, aid resources; but more often than not these people have come round to my way of thinking before I have had time to put finger to keyboard. More crucial has been my using the column as a weapon in my life-and-death struggle with the Pac-men of HIV. HIV may be able to mutate out of reach out of any drug or drug combo you throw into its maw, but it cannot type. So I can tell all the world – well, OK, the nation – what horrors it is now getting up to, and it cannot mutate fast enough to learn to use a PC and write an opposing column (presumably in *The Sunday Times*).

As my sight has dwindled to an accumulation of blurs (thanks to another virus – cytomegalovirus, a senior of the herpes family) I am increasingly house- and desk-bound. But that doesn't mean I'm out. Not yet, not for a while. And even as it thinks of more diseases of cats, sheep and pigeons to throw at me (predictable tactics for a virus believed to have jumped from a central African monkey), I will be here to tell you about it. Maybe we should rename the column Whistleblower.

1994

16 April 1994

My days as an acronym

Happy New Year! I'm sorry if this seasonal greeting wrong-foots you. I have not changed religion, switched nationality or joined a New Age caravan of perpetual dawnings (or is that awnings?). It's just that 1994 only started for me a few weeks ago, when I made the first tentative steps from my sickbed (my sofa actually) to my television (to retrieve my remote control). And while for many of you 1994 is now entering the exuberant adolescence of spring, for me this premature baby is only just learning to breathe outside the incubator. Furious at being left behind, worried about being left out, sick of being left alone, I am starting my year now. Surely April is a more appropriate month for the start of a new year? Why would anyone want to start a year in January, when the bank account is drained, the mood is sapped, the sap is frozen (as in fact is the bank account) and the next event on the socio-religious horizon is Lent? After a time of giving comes the time of giving up. Personally I just gave in.

Caved in is perhaps better, especially since I have since been told that all my problems are stress-related. Of course they are also HIV-related, but it seems that the immune system is locked in an inextricable embrace with the immense system of work, money and anxiety. I was treading the treadmill of life like some psychological Stepmaster, but instead of exercising my upper lobes and building a bright new brain, I was undermining my defences.

Eventually my mines exploded.

Now that I have reached my acronymia (the moment in anyone's life when they find themselves reduced to three initials), I can see a pattern emerging like a life and death game of Boggle. I have 'progressed' from HIV to PWA (person with Aids). I blame this on the PWE (Protestant work ethic) with which I was indoctrinated by the PTA (parent–teacher axis). My function is to avoid PCP and KNC (a.k.a. MAI) while living on a diet of AZT and DDC. QED.

While I may sound blasé about reaching this point of spellcheck *redux*, it has been a long journey out of denial (by the way, is it just me or is everyone in denial these days and where were they before? And have you noticed the similarity between in denial and eau-de-Nil and doesn't this worry you?). I didn't feel ready for change. In the seven years since the diagnosis of my 'conversion' (a stupid PC word that makes us sound like evangelical plumbers), which I actually date back to NYC 1983, I had grown accustomed to life under the sign of the plus. It was my cross to bear and I bore it without boring others. My cell count hovered in the upper two hundreds, I suffered occasional fungal flowerings, but in every other aspect my life was uninhibited by anything more serious than a condom.

Then suddenly my count began to slide. Then it began to drop. It finished with a plummet. I developed large purple stains on my legs. The fungal flowerings bloomed into itchy acne, the sort that never lets you forget it's there and that if you touch it, it will grow. Still I smiled and joked about a late youth while pursuing youths late into the night. I stifled a grimace as incipient haemorrhoids became overt (i.e. they hurt) and sat gingerly on only the softest furnishings. Still I was determined that these were all temporary inconveniences, incommodious (especially the haemorrhoids), but not irreparable. Then I got shingles.

Now of course shingles is no rarity. I have been bonding with a list of shinglers across the globe, from the theatre director in Surrey (who took eight weeks to recover) to the movie producer in Hollywood (*Lassie*, *Wind in the Willows*) who feared losing his sight. And before you pooh-pooh the whinnies of a man whose next film could cause havoc among your children's soft toys, just last week I had a letter from my oldest best friend in Australia who has suffered two bouts of shingles in one year and lost the sight in one eye. While he talks bravely of monocles, of positive thinking and daily worship at the shrine of the great god Zovirax, I recently tried walking to the bathroom with one eye closed and am still nursing my bruises.

So let us be clear. Shingles may be the older brother to chickenpox, but this is no chicken-shit affair. This is the real war of nerves. If you had to choose where to have an infection that lurked within your system and was on constant recall every time you overstepped the hidden stress-excess barrier, you wouldn't choose your nerve endings as the best location.

But that is herpes zoster for you. I, of course, was not satisfied with the normal skin-deep shingles on the arms, chest and face. I had to go one better and swallow the barbed wire. My shingling was interior pebble-dashing. I got it in my guts.

On New Year's Eve, in a distant Scottish castle, after an elaborate curry washed back with some juvenile wine and crowned with a senile cognac, I succumbed to a slight pain in my side. The minor sideburn. I thought I would sleep on it. That is my solution to most such crises. It is a good way of resolving problems and making friends. But by the next day I had developed the pained expression of someone who has just remembered that John Major is still prime minister. By the end of the day, as my friends hopped around the house in the throes of synthetic ecstasy, I was lying in front of the fire in unnatural agony, clutching pillows, chewing table legs, unravelling rugs and wondering whether being in the fire wouldn't be less painful. Ten days, two hospitals, two aeroplanes, one ambulance, three doctors, one drip and twenty thousand jabs of pethidine later, my bottom resembled an abandoned pincushion, my body resembled the 'before' photograph in the 'they used to kick sand in my face' adverts, but I had a diagnosis. I had shingles in my bowels.

Suddenly I was rushed out of the main ward into my own room with my own en suite bathroom (pretty pointless as the last three weeks of opiate dependence had left bowel movements as distant a memory as the Labour movement, and as potentially painful as the movements of labour). I was connected to a morphine pump, an acyclovir drip and a direct-dial telephone line. And then it began to dawn on me – as fast as anything can when the world is glimpsed from behind morphine curtains – that I was no longer just a positive person. My T-cells were ex-cells. I was in a bed in an Aids ward and my main communication with the outside world was via Interflora. As my mother so succinctly put it: 'Oh, my God. I suppose this is the beginning!' I had become a PWA, even if I felt more like a PWTA (person with tummy-ache) and at times more like a TAWP (tummy-ache with person).

So it has started, the Mortal Kombat video game of my life. I have the armoury – vitamins, amino acids, acupuncturists. Everything from now on is a test of skill and nerve . . . and luck. Stick with me on this one. I'm getting good at this.

14 May 1994

A rash of easy promises: giddy with pain and giggling with tickles, I would have swallowed swords and eaten fire if someone had whispered that it had worked for them. And there is always someone for whom it worked

This morning I am shuddering slightly. I have just tipped a half-pint of tepid pond water down the sink and spat out the mouthful I had just gulped.

I am not sure whether the spasms still racking me are the aftershocks of aftertaste, or a religious exorcism. I am not sure of anything right now. I am, as they say, between faiths. Medicine is all about belief – belief that what you are doing, taking, injecting, swallowing, is going to do some good. Over the past few months, I have learned to believe very strongly in morphine. I have since emerged from that dark cult, but I am still stumbling in and out of the broad church (hospital) into odd little chapels (clinics) seeking the miracle cure that will restore my energy, appetite, breath, T-cells and youth.

The pond water only looked, smelt and tasted like a fetid puddle. It was, in fact, a Chinese herbal tea it had taken an hour and a half of soaking and boiling to brew. But I like my religion to be sweet 'n' low church, not too stringent or astringent. This was more like a monastic routine of mortification. I was on day four of a ten-day regime and wobbling.

I had sought the sanctuary of the Cherry Blossom Clinic only a few days previously in a state of intense agitation. I genuinely could not sit still.

I had woken up to discover that my skin had erupted. I was no longer a pink person. I had entered my crimson period. My back was one vast red blotch. My legs a mess of measles. My arms a fretwork of red freckles. My feet were weal-heeled and my hands were speckled. Even my face – and hitting the face is really aiming below the belt – was a welter of lumps.

Actually, I was spared the full flush of this rash blush as a severe viral conjunctivitis had reduced my vision to that of a man driving through a tropical rainstorm with no windscreen wipers. But even if I could only blink at my new complexion, the itching had me skipping a little St Vitus's dance round a sequence of hospital waiting rooms.

I cannot fault my doctors. Within hours, I was quivering in dermatology as balms were prescribed to keep me calm. I was given tubes of ointment for my body and face, little green pills to deflate the inflammations and large green sachets to empty into my bath. But, even now, I didn't believe. I couldn't accept that creams and pills would do the trick. So, as I sat basted in Dermovate, my face sticky with Eumovate, my bath full of oleates, I rang the Cherry Blossom.

Desperate men seek desperate remedies. My conversion, like that of the born again, was conducted in a state of hysteria. Giddy with pain and giggling with tickles, I would have swallowed swords and eaten fire if someone had whispered that it had worked for them. And there is always someone for whom it worked who will give you a number and an address and send you into the strange world of quick quack cures. I know because I have been there before.

Do not misunderstand me. I have not turned my back on the herbal world or the ancient remedy. I would walk across hot coals to be punctual for my acupuncturist and meditation has proved a stimulating tranquillizer. But I have also been waylaid by false prophets seeking quick profits from easy promises. I have been led by and have paid through the nose.

There was the kindly lady of Mildmay Park, who listened to my tales of woe – my boyfriend had dumped me just as I started dumping T-cells – and then slipped a pill under my tired tongue and left us both to dissolve on the 73 bus. There was the valkyrie of Earl's Court who rubbed my feet with electrodes and told me not to eat oranges, chocolate, wheat, butter, milk or cheese while prescribing a regimen of drops and pills – three of one to be taken twice a day for one week, and two of the other three times a day for two weeks, and then one of another four times a day for one week – that would have left twenty pill-free minutes per twenty-four-hour day. I still have the pills, but not the £90 fee.

And then there was Dr Blanchard's Tibetan clinic. I arrived there in great distress – which is a kind of Kensington word for pain. The clinic was full of distressed Kensingtonians for whom a pain was the news that nanny might quit and who used the clinic to kill time and, where possible, the traces of its passing. But in among the Barbours and pearls there were those whose faces bore more than the pitterpatter of tiny crows' feet, whose eyes winced and flinched at more than an unsatisfactory horoscope.

I was one such. I was in pain. I was exhausted. I was at my wits' end with my guts. Dr Blanchard took me into a room and looked into my eyes and said, 'You have a three-inch lesion in your lower intestine.' Now, people have looked into my eyes before and said, they are blue, they are intelligent, they are bloodshot. But even if they thought they could see into my soul they never pretended to see into my bowels.

A well person might have laughed and walked away. I gasped and sat down, and when Dr Blanchard said, in that caring, sharing way, 'You know, Oscar, it's all right to cry,' I had to fight against the full Pavlovian flood.

For the first few sessions (he did, of course, need to see me three times a week for one hour for the next eighteen months at £20 a session, £50 for the treatments and a special first-consultation price of £35), I believed in my new healer, with his penetrating eyes. He stuck needles in my head that heated my feet and had assistants wave hot herbs over my chill chest. But as I got better, he got bored. As his attentions faded so did my faith.

My treatment declined into being left alone in a dark room for half an hour, which gave me too much time to read the certificate on the wall, conferring Blanchard with the doctorate of the International Open University of Complementary Medicine of Colombo. Colombo? Careful enquiries revealed that this university was, in fact, a backstreet acupuncture clinic in a suburb of the Sri Lankan capital that dispensed doctorates with the same flair as it had distributed professorships.

I did not turn. My faith had been broken. And once the faith lapses the cure collapses. Now I do not suggest that Dr Guang Xi of the Cherry Blossom Clinic is anything other than a skilled herbalist, but the truth is that by the time I went to see her the Dermovate had done its work and the rash had faded to faint purple traces. I'm like those people who suddenly find God in moments of panic. Without an affliction I need a miracle – but not one that tastes of pond water. I am back in the broad church of mainstream medicine . . . until the next crisis of confidence brings its crisis of conscience.

11 June 1994

The virtues of bad habits

I feel disgustingly well. Actually, this morning I also feel disgusting but this is not a medical problem. It is an eating and drinking problem, and if I am honest a bit of a smoking problem too. Eyebrows are probably even now rising, eyes rolling, tongues tut-tutting. How can a responsible, intelligent, young (I don't make these lists up) man with a life-endangering condition further endanger his life with such pointless and cheap (so not entirely pointless) abuses?

Why isn't he taking the good advice of that nice young man Brinley Mitchell (Letters, 7 May) and climbing rocks and sailing boats and generally beaming inward with self-love, instead of hanging out in late-night smoke-filled haunts littered with weary *demi-mondaines* sipping the last chance vodkatini and retelling tall stories of when he met Madonna ('s brother).

Well, I'm sorry, but we all choose our lives and it would take more than a spiritual refurbishment to risk mine on a vertical rock face. I have always taken the view that mountains are there for just that – the view. There is the one of the mountain and the one from the mountain and if the latter requires scrambling for toeholds up a slab of sheer granite then I'm happier at the bottom looking up.

As for sailing; well, I'm sorry but, as Sinead would say, among the things I have not got I have not got a yacht. Careless of me I admit. But, Brinley, I'm always happy to visit yours. Just do not ask me to help you sail it. And please make sure the wind is down, the sun is up and those booms don't keep zooming across the sun deck just as I raise my head to change the tape in the Walkman.

My point is that life is what you want it to be and now that I am back to life I am returning to many of my favourite bad habits and habitats. To quote the immortal words of the sadly mortal Phil Lynott, 'the (sick) boy (sic) is back in town'.

I now, like Brinley, expect health. In fact, as one of the 'me first, me too, me me me' generation (older brothers and sister to Generation X, a.k.a. the 'who me? oh shit' generation) I demand health. But it took time to get over being ill. Being ill can become a dangerous addiction. For three months I prefaced and interrupted every conversation with the line, delivered in a sort of wincing *sotto voce*, 'Well, of course, I don't know if you know, but I haven't been very well.' I loved the faux humility of it, the pretence at self-effacement while demanding instant attention and gentle reverence.

But even as my faded tones seized sympathy and wrenched concern, this pallid routine began to pall. My catchphrase had caught me out. I was becoming one of the professionally sick. I was planning medical retirements, a life of waiting rooms and repeat prescriptions.

I had acquired a series of flinching tics intended to communicate intense and private pain to the others in the supermarket, building society or cinema queue (they simply flinched back and failed to budge). I had retreated behind the curtains of my morphine and was lolling in my sick room waiting for the camellias to grow. All I was lacking was Zeffirelli's set dresser and Dirk Bogarde's tailor.

But I was growing sick and tired of being sick and tired. And having made my bid for constant attention, I was furious to find myself left alone and increasingly left out. I was outside the perimeter fence staring through the chain link of my sick room window as life went on the other/out side.

Of course people made detours off the beaten track to visit me in my cul-de-sick (sic), but they were only visiting. They delivered cards and flowers and gossip, but they were like messengers from a far-off land who had to return before the sun (or my stomach) turned. Where they had life to go back to, all I had was the sofa and the remote control.

So, sick of myself and my selfishness, I took control and went to California, the Magic Kingdom where everything is just fine as long as you're not too black, too Spanish, too poor, too rich, too scared or too brave.

It was Venice that changed me. Venice, California, that is. While Dirk died on the Lido, Oscar revived on a Lilo. I fled London in a pilgrimage to the sun, and before you start muttering about melanomas and premature ageing (not a major concern and in any event a tautology) I will confess to being a sun-head. I love the sun. I do not lie in it; I get too bored and too queasy. And I do not fake it; sunbeds tend to turn me a kind of toasted orange. But for the delicate sensitive little flower (flower, that is, not weed) I had become, the sun was my life-supply. I am sure I have photosynthetic brain cells. And it worked. I flourished. I blossomed. I bloomed.

After two weeks I left LAX a transformed creature. Pumped up on Muscle Beach punches, munching on amino acids and carrying my own bags I strode across the concourse, still flinching, but now I was in control. I had repossessed my body and the euphoria was proving an anaesthetic.

I hadn't climbed any rocks or circumnavigated any capes, but I had drunk wheatgerm and ginger concentrate, cycled to slap-up breakfasts of oatmeal and scrambled eggs, swum ever increasing laps in an open-air pool and eaten sun-dried vegetables on sun-soaked patios on Sunset Boulevard.

And now I am back, living my life as I liked to live it. I am sure that Brinley is right, that positive thinking leads to a sunny disposition, but I do know that all the people I know who died, died of a disease not a bad mood. So I am not going to try and control my pulse with pulses or kow-tow to brown chow; in any case, for this body Beanz Meanz the Runz.

But I am bodybuilding on calorie powerpacks and pigging out on Haägen-Dazs in a 'controlled' experiment to gain weight. I am thundering through all three courses on the menu and saying yes to the late-night *digestif* (after all, alcohol is fattening, isn't it?).

And yes, in giddy, forgetful moments before, during and at the end of the meal I light a cigarette and pretend – like a hundred million others – that nothing is wrong. But before you write me off as just another PWA Patsy, I do exercise hard, sleep well and depilate regularly. And I am happy. Happy to be alive and well enough to enjoy it.

There is only one problem. I seemed to have passed my weight-gain target and I'm having a problem finding the brakes. This erstwhile lean Love Muscle is developing soft-covered love handles. Oh well. Pass the Belgian chocolate while I think what to do.

9 July 1994

A libido stuck in limbo

Can we talk about it? Does it bother you? It seems to bother a lot of people and it is beginning to bother me. You know what I'm talking about. You don't? Where have you been for the last two weeks. Indoors? You haven't been in this sun? You haven't seen what it does to people? You haven't felt what it does to you? Don't get huffy. It's time we faced up to this one. I'll say it first and then you can just join in. OK. Here goes. SEX.

I have to talk about sex, because the sun has left me brimming with volatile hormones and promiscuous enzymes. I am almost drowning in unspent sap or, as my friend David Huggins would say, I am suffering a bad case of DSB (deadly sperm build-up). But the problem with sex is I get the feeling that I'm not even supposed to think about it. 'You're sick, honey. Sex is over. It's the sperm that's deadly, not the build-up. Take up reading or macramé.' A friend of mine, after nearly dying from a rare bowel disorder and being fitted with a temporary colostomy bag, asked the ward sister what she recommended for sex. She wasn't asking the nurse to recommend new partners. After all, she is a happily married woman. She just wanted to know how other people managed to make whoopee without bursting the bag or twisting the tube. 'Most people in this situation are not thinking about sex, madam,' said the nurse with the granite-hipped piety of one for whom sex has never been an issue (or at most the occasional tissue).

My case does not involve a bag – I do not have any strapped-on accessories.

I am not good at accessorizing anyway. But I, too, am supposed to be beyond sex. The trouble is that sex is not beyond me. It was for a while. I know I keep harking on about morphine, but it was the most significant part of my life for several weeks. But apart from condemning me to a life of sofa-bound torpor, my daily diet of pink and purple pills also seemed to leave me numb. Well, of course, that was the point. To kill the pain. But the numbness extended beyond the pain into my seldom reached-for nether reaches.

For a while I didn't even notice the difference. Morphine kills the desire as well as the ability. It is very efficient like that. But then I began to remember bits of a pre-torpid past, days of sit-ups, press-ups and sudden unexpected stick-ups. I toyed a little with these memories and a little more, but with no result.

I escaped the morphine by running away to California, land of beaming sunshine and gleaming pectorals. This should have been my great sexual reawakening. But Los Angeles enacts a form of contraception by intimidation.

It is, in fact, always a relief to come back to Europe and

find that there are normal, lanky, misshapen, oddly sorted and mismatched people in the world.

Southern California is a kind of supermodel production line. And the awful truth is that even the bimbos have MBAs, watch European films and have cycled no-hands across the Gobi with only Kierkegaard for company. So while one would love to dismiss every body-builder as a no-brain gym-dandy, one is instead thrown back on the old Euro-snobbery that over-achievement (in life, work or musculature) is vulgar. We can, of course, all enjoy a good giggle at the expense of the muscle-bubble steroid-queen waddling down the street with his feet two metres apart to avoid the discomfort of chafing thigh rub.

But for every inflated pill-popper and buttock-jabber, high on someone else's (or something else's) hormones, there are another ten lean-contoured, bronzed and effortlessly blond Rhodes scholars cycling off for a meeting with their personal trainer-manager-chef. It kills me. Moreover, it kills any desire or ability to remove any piece of clothing in a public place. And remember that on this visit I was over a stone under weight, pale grey in complexion and weak in both leg and spirit.

Since then, I have returned to London and resumed my relationship with my Spanish photographer in Brussels. But while my lover has succeeded in reaching my nethers, we do live in different countries. This means long weekends together and longer weeks apart: it's as if we are being EC regulated according to post-Gatt quotas.

Our erogenous zone has become the telephone receiver. But while I heartily endorse safe sex, sex with no physical contact at all is like eating fast food. You have the idea of pleasure but none of the sensation. Now this is not some plea for guilt-free infidelity. I am not invoking the promiscuity clause in the buggers' charter and calling on my right to tart, tramp and troll. I don't think I could face a return to the bad old days of pub crawls, bar hops and limp clubs. There is too much to get past and through and beyond before you can get naked. There is the pre-sex chat, the pre-sex tea and, too often, the pre-sex run like hell. My sitting room is the aphrodisiac equivalent of cod-liver oil. The seats are stiff-backed and hard-bottomed. Moments brinking on passion in public places become suddenly tense and coy. As we sit, wordlessly sipping strained tea, sex seems to drain away, and men leave without leaving a stain.

Before you write me off as a lonely singlet on the singles scene, I should come clean: forget the dirt, all I want is the right to flirt. But every time I wink, nod, smile or moon at a stranger, I feel I have started something I cannot finish.

How can I take someone home and then explain the large purple marks on my legs and arms, the rows of pill bottles by the bedside and the sudden midnight dashes to the loo? You may think, like my friend's matron, that I am simply being silly. But, as Edna would say, I have drives and juices, and in the summer I get swamped.

But there's no fun in flirting if you know you can't follow it through, or at least follow it home. Of course, I have sex with my boyfriend. We all do.

Well, you know what I mean. And I could have sex with strangers in the dark corners of multi-storey sex parks. We all have done. But sex is not really it. Not the crux. It's the chase, the hunt, the tally-ho (a.k.a. the loiter).

It's risky, dangerous and, most of the time, leads nowhere. After all, half our winks, nods and furtive smiles are directed at men who would happily break our teeth, arms and best china. But it's the best game in town, and I feel disqualified.

Of course, the problem is all in my head. You are how you feel, not what you feel. But, while I'm wrestling with sexual conundrums, could someone solve a short-term problem for me? It's not much to ask. It would just make it easier to think if all the workmen in the street kept their shirts on.

6 August 1994

A horizontal road to hell

I long for the vertical. To be able to stand and move freely among the standing, walking people. But I seem to have developed an irreversible horizontal. I think it all started in Minorca. Loath as I am to blame that pretty, quiet island with its startling clear water and devastatingly hot sun for anything more than a deep tan. But that is where I first went face down.

I felt a bit guilty at first. It seemed so strange to be getting up in the morning just to lie down next to the pool, and then to leave the pool for a brisk lunch of tomatoes and onions in order to depart for the beach to lie down again. But I quenched my guilt by looking around me at the assorted and entirely recumbent Spaniards, English and Germans for whom the short journey from the beach to the sea seemed to be all they (or I) could muster. This I call lying down for pleasure and, given that I was with my Spanish photographer, occasionally it was lying down for very great pleasure.

However, on my return I discovered a whole different kind of lying down: lying down because I couldn't stand up. I was all right at first, although I had known something was wrong since the morning of my departure from Minorca as I took a shave and came across a gland, a gland, that is, that hurt to touch. This was quite intriguing to me as I have never felt very certain of my glands – where they are or what they feel like. But I guessed it boded ill; I just had no idea quite how ill. I was all right for the first day, but by the second I was in such a state of confusion that I managed to fall asleep in almost every room in the house. But I gamely trotted off to work, rather red eyed, but deep tanned and determined to keep my end up. I kept it up until five o'clock that afternoon when, after a long-scheduled *Kaleidoscope* interview about lesbian films, I fled the all too sonorous declamations of 'Chris Dunkley of the *Financial Times*' – a man so confident of his opinions he seems equally confident of our opinions of his opinions – for the outpatients at the Middlesex.

I love the Middlesex – they see you immediately, make rapid decisions, then act on them. This is far from true elsewhere. I spent a week of wintry hell in a Glasgow hospital where a test was discussed for a day, happened the day after and the results were unlikely to 'come down' within two days.

Meanwhile, black-shod, white-uniformed nurses marched the ward with the grimly disapproving look of people who had been left the naughty boys to look after. On one occasion, the most brutal and Presbyterian of them all told me I shouldn't be in the bath because that bath had been reserved for a patient who was sick. Whether I didn't qualify as sick because I was an HIV gay Sassenach or because I wasn't having an amputation and didn't have a temperature, I don't know and couldn't ask in my shampooed and naked fury as I slammed the door in her face. But at moments of playful revenge I have dismantled this woman and reassembled her back-to-front in my head.

The doctor at outpatients took one look at me and what was now the goitre round my neck and simply said: 'Are you ready to be admitted?' I nodded like one of those dogs in the back of a car. I was already totally submitting control. For three days I had put on a brave face, but it was cracking up and I felt very strange.

After a short examination, he told me I had a very high fever and he was admitting me immediately. I took my brown envelope and drifted helplessly to the ward where, within minutes, I was wrapped in a warm bed with a thermometer in my mouth and one of those inflatable blood-pressure bags squeezing my arm. And then the hell started.

Initially we – well, I – had thought it was simply a case of attacking the goitre and everything else would clear up. Well, the goitre quite wisely got out of there fast, but my temperature began to zoom around like the ball on the pinball machine. It would drop to 38° and everyone would look hopeful and then it would rocket to 40°, leaving me prostrate and burning alive. People would ask, enthusiastically, whether I had good hallucinations. I didn't.

Occasionally, the whole room would take a jump to the left or the right as if I were learning some barn dance, and sometimes, as I closed my eyes for another night of tormented sleep and dreams about hospitals, the room seemed to be filling with smoke. But nothing you could really enjoy.

But the worst thing was not knowing what was wrong, because I had to lie there like a slow-grilling chicken while doctors raced cultures to and from labs and looked depressed and worried every time they took the thermometer out of my mouth. I couldn't even do anything to alleviate my boredom, nervousness and lurking despair because every time I picked up a book I fell asleep. I was reduced to the level of the *Evening Standard* and *Hello!*. That is the first thing you have to learn as a patient. Patience.

And then, in the middle of all this, the diarrhoea hit. Now we have all had diarrhoea, but this was the infernal version. As soon as I had made one bolt from bed to bathroom, I needed to go again. I could normally hold off for about ten minutes before that gurgle became too ominous. As a result, I have probably developed some strange new muscles from all the clenching which, I dare say, will become useful at some unexpected moment in later life.

Racked by temperatures that kept rising as if testing the capacity of the thermometer, dehydrated by runs that had me dashing backwards and forwards, I lay back and said to any available deity: 'This couldn't be any worse, could it?' Clearly, I upset someone because by the next day I had a choking cough to match all those around me. Then suddenly, the world changed – they found the bug that was giving me the septicaemia, the morphine killed the diarrhoea and the cough dried up. I was left with nothing more serious than excruciating midafternoon headaches.

Ever the impatient in-patient, I started a campaign for my release which was finally, warily indulged with the proviso that I came in every day for an injection. In two days' time, I shall take my first weak and wobbly steps into the world of fast-moving things and independence.

Having longed to escape, I know I shall miss this place with its smart, friendly nurses and thoughtful, attentive doctors. I shall certainly hate having to cook for myself, but at least I won't have to have dinner at 5.30 p.m., and watching *The Singing Detective* won't be so hard. As far as I see it, I've just won round three. Now I just need time to get my strength back to fight round four . . . whenever that may be. Why don't we just cancel it?

3 September 1994

Headache? Tense, nervous headache?

It's arrived! It's not too heavy. Intermittent, but not quite regular. And it's mostly front-loading, which is easier. It's principally a left-eye variant, rising to upper cranium. I can see and speak and hear through it. I can probably wash up through it, and yet it will mean perfectly justified sessions of lying down and 'meditating' through it.

The arrival of the day's headache has become the great tension of my mornings, as I wait for the various false leads – the don't move your head to the left or right headache, the don't smile or raise an eyebrow headache – to settle down. One needs a certain patience and sang-froid in these cases, because some of the early-morning manifestations can be shocking enough to send nervous eyes glancing to the bottle of morphine sulphate crowned with its syringe. If the nerve trembles as a wave of high-intensity total head glove grip threatens, the best thing is to carry the aspirin bottle (soluble) around the house until it has cleared.

But until you have established which headache is the day's choice, and at what intensity, with what special side features (extra temple pain on the hour, neck paralysis at moments of emotion), and what intermittence, you cannot develop an equilibrium. You are stuck in the Pain Anticipation Zone, a tense purgatory that some say brings its own pain, arguing that the fidgety hyperconcentration on every minor twinge, spasm or wave creates its own headache.

Personally, I think this is headache sceptics talking. Pain Anticipation is a problem. You can, if not careful, find yourself simply sitting waiting for the next thump and get caught in eddies of echo blows, seismic fallout from the previous punch. However, it should not be indulged. It is possible, as the morning passes, to train yourself to concentrate on other things than the imminence of the next wince. Ask yourself serious questions as you move gingerly around the house: Where's the milk? How does the fridge open? Why can't I see straight? God it hurts when I bend over, is that a headache or just an unpleasant position? Of course, it is hard at this time of day to be certain of anything, as many of us will still be recovering from the overnight headache – the B52 five-second fly-past or the Stealth cluster bomber and air display acrobatic team – and are probably suffering a few errant fly-pasts.

Not that I am claiming to be an expert. I am a neophyte when it comes to the headache business. I was holding forth at a dinner last night on the difference between the drowning in syrup headache (heavy head, no air, permanent pain, try and blame the weather if only for personal comfort), and the visiting flashes headache (sudden wince and sometimes yelp-inducing pain of savage sharpness that seems to be visiting from another waveband), when the man opposite me wearily interrupted to explain that there were six versions of the gatecrashing flasher and the drowning head at least offered the benefits of consistency.

I immediately confessed to being a beginner, a recent arrival in this tortured frowning world of flinching and sighing and gentle forehead rubbing. In our family, headaches were Mother's. She had them and we tiptoed round them. There were two main varieties, the most common was the winter Sunday afternoon version which involved total blackout upstairs and a silence mandate downstairs. This was impossible for all three kids to observe. We would sit round the dining room table playing our games in whispers, and then the giggles would start and pass like fire from brother to sister, rising in volume until the dreaded voice from upstairs bellowed from the dark some incoherent threat/demand, and my father would appear, breathless and nervy, to insist that we stop laughing and enjoy ourselves . . . quietly.

The other version was the Holiday Classic. This usually came midway through any holiday and was an instant liberator, as with five people in one caravan it is very hard to insist on silence. Instead, my father went into pious potter – administering the occasional pill (the word codeine has a particular resonance from my childhood) and fidgeting in a confined space while we were left to run amok.

I, meanwhile, had a blissfully headache-free life. Occasionally a small pain would lead me to ask in a plaintive voice for an Anadin as if headaches conferred a kind of intellectual prestige. Now I know. They just confer life-eroding pain. They began when I first left hospital, prematurely, some would say arrogantly. Liberty flashed before my eyes and I smiled, and then the smile turned crooked and snapped as a boot kicked a hole in my head. The boot was followed by a steam train, a brick, another boot and then a whole succession of heavy and aggressive objects.

Within seconds I was face down on my bed, moaning strange prayer-curses into my pillow. I knew that that was today gone. I'd had headaches during the last days in hospital, but somehow, awash with painkillers and antibiotics, I had blamed the drugs, and the drugs had prevented me from thinking any further. Now, in the warm light of a summer's day, the sun hit the corner of my head (principally left eye with cranium rising) with a savage Doc Marten (steel-capped) and left me floored until the next day when exactly the same attack would occur.

Tearfully and penitently, I returned to hospital, only three days after having made my grand exit, curled up in my bed in the corner of the ward and commenced to groan, moan and shriek with every spasm. I had decided that stiff upper lips were for stiff little twits and I was going to let the ward (and the rest of the world) know the depth, frequency and cruelty of my pain.

To their credit, the Middlesex leapt into action – in one night I had three scans and a lumbar puncture. But they found nothing, and two weeks later, muted and moderated by beta blockers, I was released back into the world.

The boots and bricks were no longer flying. It was back-street knitting needles now, and sudden little slashes with rusty penknives. But these were easier to accommodate.

That is what I do now. I accommodate my headaches. My

only problem is a shortage of furniture. I cannot find anything between soluble aspirin (comfortable but not durable) and morphine sulphate (comfortable but not sensible). People have been popping names at me from Nurofen to Hedex, but I think it might be time to watch some serious TV ads. Except that it always brings on a back-head clincher with front flashes and late-night side-winders. Oh. My head.

1 October 1994

When the top of the world disappeared

I should be dancing round the mulberry bush in jubilation. My headaches have lifted. Bar the occasional late-night twinge, probably induced more by the quality than the quantity of television I have been watching, I am pain-free. I can even identify the moment of liberation: sitting at a table playing cards in Soho at a friend's house, I suddenly felt as if someone had removed a rather tight-fitting helmet from my head. My brain resumed breathing and a smile crept irresistibly across my face.

I say I should be dancing round the mulberry bush but unfortunately I am having a hard time actually finding the bush and dancing is out of the question as even my walking has taken on the lopsided gait of the afternoon drunkard. I have not become a secret drinker – in fact my reaction to alcohol these days is that of a twelve-year-old who tries his mother's wine at the dinner table and runs from the room with a hand over his mouth. I blame this on one or other of the drugs that I am or have been or will be taking, which has/have also destroyed chocolate (turning the flavour to industrial rubber) and cigarettes (the smoke is now so acrid I can smell someone smoking on the other side of Charing Cross Road).

The problem is my eyes. When I had shingles inside my guts, back in the winter of this *annus miserabilis*, I believed that pains in the stomach were the worst possible affliction man could suffer; that the stomach was the body's fulcrum and therefore amplified and spread all pain it endured throughout the body like a radio transmitter. Then came the headaches and I adjusted my opinions upwards. The head was the tenderest part of the whole corpus (careful spelling required here), and any pain it suffered paralysed the whole.

But there is something about eyes that beats everything else for vulnerability. I am more protective of my eyes than most men are of their groins. I wince, flinch and mutter imprecations every time someone in a movie gets it in the eye. *King Lear* is out of the question. So it took a lot of restraint to keep calm when half the vision in one just vanished. It was very sudden. I was in Edinburgh, shivering in front of the television in a borrowed apartment as rain fell horizontally outside. It was Festival time again. But I was finding it hard to concentrate. A blur had appeared at the edge of my right eye that would not be rubbed away, but instead grew like the shadow of a very shaggy eyebrow. I tried the old optician's trick of holding one hand over one eye and looking through the other to discover that my right eye barely functioned. Gaping grey holes turned its images into meaningless patchworks. I'm stoned, I thought, and went back to my tea and Madeira cake.

The next morning I opened my eyes and saw half the day breaking through half the window. Of course it wasn't really that bad. Like an instant art restorer, the brain does a lot of filling in and retouching, but the blur hovered still, naggingly like a visible hangover.

If I closed my good eye the tops of people's heads disappeared along with the sky, roofs and low-flying birds. If I turned to look over my right shoulder a sudden attack of vertigo sent me reeling and any sudden movement of the head caused instant whiplash. I could read if I ignored the ghost words floating about the page, and the television did eventually come into focus (it was nothing a good thump on the side couldn't cure) but walking – already a problem for someone whose legs had been turned to Twiglets by four weeks in a hospital bed – was hazardous. I could see short-term prospects, like puddles and pillar-boxes, but any attempt to look at the bigger picture, the street ahead say, left me wobbling close to a topple.

This was not good news. I didn't know yet whether it was bad news but I knew that bad news could be really bad. I knew, or have known, enough people whose eyesight had been eaten away by CMV, the Pac-man of herpes viruses, to know that this could be it. I also knew that this Pac-man chomps at terrifying speed. But, a few hundred miles from my doctor, I decided to blame the pot (which we had finished the night before) and to add marijuana to my list of things I would no longer touch.

It didn't stop raining until Doncaster, but thereafter grew sunnier and sunnier as we approached London, so by the time we arrived at King's Cross my mood was as filthy as a Princes

Street puddle. I hate being somewhere else when the sun is shining – whether it's indoors, in bed or in Scotland.

But the sun did seem to restore some of my eroded eyesight and when I got home I decided that the problem was passing.

The following day it was worse. I collided with the door jamb while trying to walk into the kitchen and had trouble locating the spoon for my cornflakes, the cornflakes with the spoon and my mouth with the cornflake-laden spoon. Not all of that was bad eyesight, of course.

The doctor held my hand when he told me that it was what I was afraid it was. The CMV had been active in my eye for about a month (my headaches? they were only a month old), and we had caught it very early. He would start the treatment there and then, he said, setting up a drip and collecting various hypodermics. Oh, and would I be checking in tonight or tomorrow morning for the three-week period? I paled (or is it blanched?). I was only two weeks out of hospital and I was being invited back for three more. This slippery slope had very small plateaux. Maybe I should have change-of-address cards printed. The nurse in attendance must have noticed my distress (my mouth opening and shutting, my pupils dilating, my arms and legs twitching) because she suggested that, if I could manage it, they could treat me just as well if I came in twice a day, and so for the last three weeks I have been a double-day dripper, shivering at the 73 bus stop at the top of Pentonville Road at 10 a.m. and 7 p.m. every day, including Sunday.

In the meantime I ask everyone I can about the long-term prognosis and everyone I ask does everything they can to avoid the question. So, it's one day and one paving stone, lamppost and errant pedestrian at a time, and if you see me weaving my way up Tottenham Court Road in a kind of erratic waltz time, you'll not accuse me of drinking. I'm just trying to get from A to B and sometimes it's nice to visit C, D and E en route.

29 October 1994

No charge for the olfactory hallucinations

Something just crawled into my mouth and died. Or at least that's what it tastes like, and that's assuming that something tasting like a dead vegetable can crawl, and, of course, assuming that just because it tastes to me like a dead vegetable that that is in fact what it tastes like. Although I am experiencing the flavour of mouldering compost on my tongue, the actual taste could be lemon soufflé with ginger snaps on the side.

I have stopped relying on my own senses to tell me anything. If I believed what they do tell me I would probably never leave the house. I recently became convinced that I smelt funny. Well, not so much funny as acrid, like some sort of chemical effluent. It was not a poisonous smell, but nor was it a natural smell and, having grown accustomed over the years to the aroma of my own body, I found it deeply disconcerting to have acquired this new flavour. But then I also knew that my sense of smell, like my sense of taste, was out of sorts. So did I smell funny or was it just that my smelling was funny?

Nobody had actually commented on my new scent – but then the English are very wary of face-to-face honesty, and suggesting that someone smells a bit off could very quickly lead to pit bulls at dawn. Even bad breath is something we turn a closed nostril to, so I could not even be sure that the fetid taste in my mouth was not wilting the buttonholes of everyone I spoke to. Instead, I was left searching people's faces for the first sign of a wince or a wrinkle, while gulping a diet of Clorets and Dettol.

Personally, I put it all down to the drugs. I have been reduced to an amalgam of side effects, running the gamut from nausea to vertigo with olfactory hallucinations as a special extra.

In theory I am relatively well. I have no fever, no pain and the CMV (cytomegalovirus) in my eyes has been arrested. But in reality I stagger from spasm to wince via belch and fart, gripping my head in consternation as another sinus cavity over-spills and my equilibrium drowns in the tidal shifts of mucus.

The flatulence I can explain – at least to myself. A steady diet of antibiotics has apparently deforested my interiors with the thoroughness of Agent Orange. Thankfully a regime of live yoghurt seems to have performed a horticultural miracle and I no longer shift awkwardly from cheek to cheek on restaurant seats while those around me blanch and press napkins to their faces. But, while my long-running war with my guts is reaching a happy conclusion, my stomach is at best unreliable and my head feels as if the combined air forces of several alien nations are loop-the-looping through my cranium. Occasionally I feel as if I am flying the planes myself, wearing rather too tight goggles, as the tubes above and below my eyes develop a sudden savage throb. I have had the curious problem of aching cheekbones (I have heard of people aching for cheekbones but rarely of cheekbones that ache) and have weathered storms on the lake in my inner ear, but more disconcerting is the feeling that my head is no longer my own.

Like the small child caught in the middle of a parental conflict, I am left helpless and paralysed as one lobe declares war on the other and smokescreens of poisonous fumes descend, bringing all synaptical activity to a fog-bound standstill. And that's just the effect of the Beconase inhaler.

But that said, I do not panic. Not in the way I used to panic. My panics were famous. Waking up on a Saturday morning that little bit later than planned, I would rapidly spin myself into a nervous pirouette as I recited all the duties and chores that had somehow to be performed in the remaining forty-five minutes before midday.

The plants had to be watered; I had to be showered and probably shaved; the dry-cleaning had to be collected, but before I did that I had to get dressed, which meant doing my exercises and then if I went to the dry-cleaner I must remember to get the paper and some milk and eggs, but then I wouldn't have enough money to buy flowers, so I'd have to go round the corner to the cashpoint and if I was going that far I might as well . . .

By the time I had finished this domino game of dos and must-dos and do-right-nows I was baring my teeth and rolling my eyes in a kind of feral rictus. Anyone who crossed my path invariably had their head chewed.

My then boyfriend developed the habit of hiding his head under the pillow when I came cursing my way up the stairs with his tea. His timidity only made me madder, so I would pick one of those nasty little fights that seem to go from nought to ninety in a millisecond but never make any progress – they just roar round and round the same tired tracks. In the end I had to apologize and sit down and have a cup of tea and make a list to regain a realistic perspective on this litany of errands.

I don't do that any more. I feel the accumulating weight of things that must be done and I just say to myself, well, one thing at a time and breakfast first. Suddenly I seem to understand the infinite stretch of the time-space continuum and how there will always be enough time to do the things that matter and how everything else can wait. Even fresh flowers can be bought on a Sunday or not bought at all.

I'd like to ascribe this new wisdom and self-control to a programme of mental reform and re-education. In truth, however, it is another side effect and must be put down to Propranolol, the little pink pills I have been taking ever since those ice-pick headaches sent me reeling backwards into hospital (again). I just don't get uptight any more. And I don't miss either the up or the tight.

The trouble is, my doctor probably won't renew my prescription when the bottle of pink pills runs out and there is only a few more days' supply left inside. After they've all been swallowed, I will be left to the criss-crossing frenzy of enemy aircraft swooping through my head, dive-bombing synaptical bridges as I fret about the strange smell of decay hanging over me and wander nervously between the kitchen and the bathroom trying to work out which needs washing first – my face or the plates – or worse still, trying to remember what it was I was trying to work out.

26 November 1994

In search of a comfortable creed

Has anyone got a surfboard they can lend me? I am bobbing out of control between peaks of anxiety and troughs of depression and before I get sunk in the slough of despond I would really like to paddle away to a new horizon.

The trouble is, I can't see that far ahead.

My eyes have turned on me. I thought everything was under control and so did my doctors, until about two weeks ago when I woke up with my head in the equivalent of a disco bubble lamp. Strange transparent amoeba drifted constantly in front of my eyes as small black thunderflies darted in random directions. Neither amoeba nor thunderflies, these were 'floaters', debris adrift in my eyeball, shaken up like the fake snow in a child's toy. My eyes, transfixed by the manic movements of these boating floaters, darted and drifted after them, leaving me distractedly colliding with door jambs, pedestrians and the occasional unforeseen tree.

Attempting to duck my sorrows if not actually drown them,

I hit the temazepam and, slumping into sleepiness, promptly sank beneath the Plimsoll line of least resistance. Weariness seemed to feed gloominess and fears gradually collected into panics. I woke up to grey days in a grey mood, the catatonics of my depression only interrupted by the palpitations of the occasional anxiety attack. Staring at the rain through my sitting room window, the drops on the glass mirrored the blurs in my eyes. I could barely raise an eyebrow let alone a smile. I seemed to have fixed my gaze on the final curtain, and, while not actually eager to peek behind it, I was suddenly losing the will to live.

My walking became erratic. My driving became a hazard. Reading was repeatedly frustrated as floaters decided to hover in my light-path, blocking out words and obscuring sentences. The only pleasure that remained was the cinema, where the images were bold and large enough to remain clear.

But after ninety minutes of staring at the screen I was left bloodshot and confused, stumbling around looking for my car, and indeed, the road.

In a state of growing terror I rang the clinic, to be told, in a voice of terrible impassivity, that the problem was probably either my retina detaching or blood leaking from tears in it. By now it was Friday evening, so, despite the apocalyptical nature of this telephone verdict, nobody was around for another two days to verify it. I spent a long, slow weekend attempting to distract myself with a steadily unsteadying succession of joints, which instead marooned me in a paranoid limbo and left my short-term memory so depleted that I forgot my PIN number and lost my cashpoint card to the spiteful clutches of the machine.

Gasping for the oxygen of optimism, all I got was the ozone of religion. A friend called by for tea on the Sunday afternoon and slipped me a Bible.

I had been looking forward to his visit, anticipating the fresh pleasures of personal empathy as an escape from the suffocations of general sympathy. For the last eighteen months he had been stricken with a virus called Epstein-Barr that left him racked with chest pains and immobilized by lethargy. Confused and scared, he fled a coke-fired lifestyle of all-night ups and postponed downs, and retired to his parents' Caribbean home for a short rest. A year and a half later he was putting a tentative toe back in London's professional waters and, while I winced a little selfishly at his determined talk of recovery, I enjoyed comparing horrors survived and reminiscing about pains now past. Cheered by the chance to relive old agonies, I grinned when he told me he had a little present for me.

I suppose I was expecting some souvenir from his Bahamanian hometown.

Instead I got this plastic-packed version of Sunday school. It wasn't even the whole Bible (it never is) – just a bowdlerized (sorry, 'revised') version of the New Testament in a pocket edition with white vinyl flexicovers and, he assured me, no thous and thees. Unfortunately, I like the thous and thees. The decorative rituals are what keep me distracted from the fact that this religion, like my insurance policies, has some pretty severe exclusion clauses that leave me damned whether I believe or not. So I'd rather take an existential punt on the essential finality of death and not sweat with terror at the prospect of hellish torments. Frankly, the earthly ones are enough.

I froze, and shortly afterwards he left, made uneasy by my talk of earlier failed flirtations with faith. Maybe I shouldn't be so suspicious, but I'm wary of anyone who peddles fantasy answers to real questions, like, Why is this happening to me? When is it going to stop? And what happens when it does? I've been avoiding these questions for the past seven years, especially the last one. Every so often someone – the benefit officer organizing my disability allowance, the counsellor questioning me about my sleeping patterns – would use the words 'terminal condition' and we would exchange a nervous glance as they looked up to see how I was dealing with the imminence of death and I looked at them to see how embarrassed they were by having to mention it. But for the most part I was intently focused on the immediate crisis, determined to deal with today before worrying about tomorrow, and avoiding altogether the Day After. I'm not keen on the idea of the afterlife – not without knowing who else will be there and what the entertainment will be. Personally I'd rather just take a rest.

But then that is my problem already. Whole weeks seem to slip by in a succession of naps. It's just that the world looks nicer with my eyes closed right now. Closing the door behind my evangelical friend, I decided to go and spend an evening with *Forrest Gump*. Maybe I was looking for a more comfortable creed. Maybe I was just trying to flee my demons. Either way, I should have known better.

The most loathed and feared dinner lady at my primary school – a woman who blue-rinsed her poodle to match her bouffant hair – used to tell me to show more gumption as I snivelled about a grazed knee or sobbed about being bullied by a boy in the year below. While I was familiar with gumption in its bottled liquid form, this more abstract philosophy needed some definition. I was certain that it involved playing football better and getting the right girls in kiss-chase, neither of which made it any more accessible.

After the first hour of the movie I was shifting in my seat and composing angry rebuttals. By the third hour I was crushed into resentful submission, intimidated by the terrifying confidence of the happy nerd. This apparently artless film is the latest and most formidable attack on all the values I have been taught to cherish – most particularly intelligence, scepticism and disobedience. Anyone questioning the strength and truth of the status quo is portrayed as a brain-addled drug addict, teetering on the brink of despair.

So, addled and teetering as I am, it is odd to find that the film has left me with a comforting maxim. As Mrs Gump is dying, a tearful Forrest asks her why this has to be and she points out the enduring truth that 'death is part of life'.

She's right. And it is oddly reassuring to be reminded that I am not alone: everyone sooner or later will go through this. What she doesn't add is that the hard thing is not being able to choose when. But then if it was left to us, how many of us would say 'Now!' too late . . . and how many too soon?

24 December 1994

The company of friends and strangers

Hope, like Alice, springs. In fact, it not only springs, it bubbles and froths like shook-up champagne and gives much the same giddy giggly rush. (I'm sorry if champagne never did that for you. It is, now, the only alcoholic drink I can stomach, so, publicly sighing with the self-sacrifice of a retiring roué, I am secretly anticipating an effervescent Christmas with all the filling of stomach and emptying of head – but ideally not the emptying of stomach via head – that goes with it.) But whatever its intoxicating properties, my hope, like the majority of supermarket mineral waters, springs from more homely sources than the vineyards of France.

Glasgow in fact.

Scotland may be the purist's chosen well from which to draw that peaty, oddly yellow water that either makes you feel you are imbibing neat minerals or that you are gargling bogwash, but Glasgow doesn't figure very highly on the Highland water diviner's divine water trail, not least because it isn't . . . high, that is. If anything bubbles out of Glasgow's gutters it is more likely to carry the aroma of twelve-year-old-whisky or that night's vindaloo challenge.

Nor has Glasgow ever figured highly on my list of ten best cities in which to develop violent pains and throw yourself at the mercy of the medics. In fact, after my (already documented) experiences with shingles – which kicked off 1994 with a boot to the guts that left me convulsed and winded in a Glasgow hospital bed, begging po-faced Presbyterian nurses for pethidine until they were convinced I was some Sassenach junkie in urgent need of 'straightening' out – Glasgow had sunk a little lower than Mogadishu (and any American city) on the list of places where I would be happy to check in to hospital.

But, as I said, hope, like water, springs from the rockiest of hard places and the recent HIV conference in Glasgow has left me with the cautious elation of one secretly inebriated at a teetotaller's Christmas party.

Suddenly the view ahead, which only last month was shrouded in the poisonous fog of depression – when it wasn't totally obscured by the mist patches of retinal floaters – seemed to clear and 1995 began to shine with the surreal glow of the Happy Valley. New drugs, fresh from successful tests, seemed to bounce into the press (albeit not quite the pharmacy) like bingo balls shooting out of a hot air vent. This was the pharmaceutical tombola in which everyone was winning prizes . . . eventually.

'Yes, ladies and gentlemen, and here's another one. This one's called 3TC and, wait for it, yes, it inhibits the spread of HIV, raises the CD4 count and goes very well with AZT. We expect a licence by February!' Before you write me off as a silly sot hooked on the buzz of fairground gambles, I assure you my optimism is laced with caution. I have had enough sobering chasers over the last year to keep my temper dry and my excitement on ice, but I had also got to the point where I couldn't see the point and was in danger of just hitting the bottle or, worse still, hitting myself with the bottle.

Of course, some of it was the weather. That's the great thing about this country. The weather is an eternally available scapegoat, because whatever it is it is never what we thought it would be, what we are used to or what we wanted. When I was hospitalized with septicaemia in July the outside world was struggling through the heat, gasping for air, trying to find the city's last viable oxygen molecule as the atmosphere turned a sulphurous yellow and cars, choking on traffic, vomited monoxides into the sweaty faces of harassed pedestrians. I lay back between my fans (electric, I'm afraid) and received a trail of bedraggled and fraught visitors, as my blood cooked up a 40° fever, my saliva evaporated and my bowels lost their grip.

In my own way, I was the perfect expression of the climatic condition.

The early autumn was all sylvan glades of brilliant shades as I strode back to health on country walks, colour flushing my cheeks to the russet of a late Cox and an early turning beech. I watched sunsets from the edge of ancient copses, scaring sheep and startling crows as I whooped with delight at the pink and blue light show. But then, inevitably, November descended like a wet blanket, shutting out the light and soaking me in drizzle even as I gawped at the Highbury Fields Guy Fawkes '*son et lumière*'. Actually, I normally like November. It has always represented the starting gate of the run-up to Christmas, the launch of a long party season kicking off on Hallowe'en and finally crashing dizzily to the floor somewhere around New Year's Eve (preferably after midnight).

But now, as the cocktail circuit leaves me dizzy, and gatherings of more than double figures leave me seeing double trying to figure out a way out, November seemed to suffocate me in damp and darkness, promising no relief until the spring. I began to envy hedgehogs their prescience, and squirrels their home storage facilities as hibernation seemed a serious option. I didn't actually want to quit. I just wanted to go to bed and get up again in another season, maybe even another country . . . Well, actually, no! Not another country.

I have not suddenly turned into a little Englander. With a Dutch mother, a Spanish boyfriend living in Brussels and the tendency to rabbit excitably (in any one of three languages) about the wonders of the Eurotunnel (and yes, I am that cutting-edge. I have been on it), I think I count as one of the leading European co-productions. But over the last year there are certain things about London that I have learned to love, cling to and never want to let go: my friends, my flat and my medics, the doctors and nurses of the Middlesex, of Mortimer Market and of i-Care, who keep putting me back together and sending me back out into the real world feeling restored, revived and ready for life, genuine life, that is, and not just some gloomy holding bay waiting for the next malaise.

I have issued paeans of praise for the Middlesex before, and as I am currently in residence at what I like to think of as my central London address (albeit cluttered with unknown flat-mates), suffering convulsive rigours from an infected portacath as my temperature soars and swoops like a fairground ride (and hoping that on this visit I can also reduce my current nipple count of twenty-three-plus to the more normal two by having the molluscum clustering round my teats deep-frozen to death), it might be politic to start with them.

There is little to say more than I have said, except that facing me across the ward are two people so sick that their only breaths seem to be chokes punctuated by vomits and their only means of communication through a mess of tubes and masks are weakly raised arms and blinking eyes. Relatives come, sit, weep and leave. Nights are disturbed. Days are barely conscious. And yet, through all this grim death rattle, the redoubtable nurses of Broderip Ward keep up an energetic cheerfulness that inspires and enthuses even the most malingering of self-pitying patients.

Hospital is never an easy place to keep a smile and, surrounded by the time-warp mirrors of people much further down the slippery slope than myself, an Aids ward can be terrifying and depressing, turning the blood to ice and the brain to mush. It is dangerously easy to slide into a state of staring inaction, watching clouds float past the window, unable even to finish the *Hello!* magazine world exclusive cover story (the September 1993 X-ray waiting room edition). But somehow the resilient gusto of these men and women, who have seen so many patients slip out of their bedridden hells into the void, remains undiminished, and their strength is contagious (for once, a welcome infection). Optimism has become my most important drug, and here, in the midst of the carnage, it is a life-saver. Low spirits lead to low resistance, and without the spirited care of the doctors and nurses, here and at the

Mortimer Market and i-Care clinics, my spirits would long since have ebbed below the healthy tidemark.

This year has also been my chance to crack the combination care code. I have entered benefit land – the world of shared care, community nursing, disabled parking permits and taxi-cards – and, while stunned and surprised to find that so much has survived the government's attempts to take everything down below the Bottomley line, I am trying to be quiet about my excitement, in case I attract too much attention and they decide to send out the Tontons Macoute of the cutback police with their budget-slashing machetes.

But I have to say that I am faring well in the welfare state, and I still marvel at how well it works. Never mind that I scarcely use my car and the taxis don't always come; there is something intensely liberating about £1.50 flat fares, and I can't help grinning about being able to park on double and single yellow lines for up to three hours and on parking meters free of charge for unlimited times.

My grin might be a little broader, however, if the traffic wardens of Westminster Council knew the rules. Cheerfully leaving my car on a parking meter behind Australia House while visiting the Courtauld (you know, Christmas shopping. My family love Impressionist masterpieces), I returned two hours later and let out a howl that mingled fury, terror and outrage.

Nobody seemed to notice, so, snatching the ticket from my windscreen, I went in search of the traffic warden responsible.

Maybe it was just as well I could not find him or her, as by now I had turned positively lupine in my rage and might simply have buried my teeth in the offending neck. Westminster – with its political cleansing, graveyard sales and general gerrymandering – is becoming London's equivalent of Queensland, a banana republic of mad bad millionaires in the middle of a more civilized city. But do they really hope to earn crucial additions to their coffers by penalizing hapless (but not hopeless) invalids? Maybe this is all part of the council's makeover policy – once they've targeted poor left-wing residents, they can start antagonizing unfit visitors.

However, all is not trouble and strife. I can slip into the quiet calm of i-Care's Islington HIV clinic and sink into the pungent pleasures of an aromatherapy massage, or sit and talk to the nurses who each week come to my house and plunge a fresh needle into my chest in a small-scale re-enactment of *Pulp Fiction* (OK, I do not look like Uma, they do not resemble Travolta or Stolz and I have not been snorting pure heroin – I try and have that injected at the hospital – but I do have a needle in my chest and how many of you can be as hip to the Zeitgeist as that?).

These people – nurses, doctors, masseurs and receptionists – have become my friends. Meanwhile, my friends have become members of the heavenly host. Before you gag on all this goodwill to all women and men (and let's face it, I am once again hip to the Zeitgeist, this being the season of inane grins and sudden tearful hugs), let me assure you that this tribute is long overdue. I will not name names (I hate to name-drop), but I must say that at times when I have doubted that life has any prospects except more and worse of the same, as the climate seemed to sink into endless night and my eyesight dwindled to an amalgam of blurs, it is the company of friends – round dinner tables from Notting Hill to Stepney Green –

that has reminded me how bon a couple of bon vivant nights can make you feel about being vivant at all.

Perhaps the classic was the world's longest Sunday lunch: a gathering of six friends round a full table in a Stepney house that started at the civilized hour of two thirty and finished at the astonishing hour of ten fifteen that evening. No, we had not been taking stimulants, nor were we trying for a British remake of *Blow Out*. This was much less about the food than about the talking . . .

and talking and talking and talking.

I stumbled off into the chill air that night feeling happier than I had any right to. The sheer warmth of human contact, the laughter and chatter, the reminiscences and the gossiping, had left me invigorated. We had not shattered any major truths or constructed any revolutionary theorems. We had simply revelled in each other's company. But as my long-term ambitions hit short-term realities and thoughts of the future became at best redundant and at worst panic-stricken, it is these evenings and these people (and not the vinyl-wrapped New Testament delivered last month by a born-again acquaintance) which have provided the meaning in my life.

And, as a coda, I must acknowledge both the love and protection of those closest to me, my family and my boyfriend, each of whom deserve chapters dedicated to their dedication. And also the encouragement of strangers – the many people who have written kind letters of solidarity, care of this column. There is a secret fraternity of sickness between people who never meet, but whose tales of hell and high water in the pursuit of temporary relief from terminal crises ,provide a mutual support. Somehow the reflection of one's own miseries in someone else's life soothes the pain of the suffering. The loneliness of illness is one of its bitterest aspects – especially as every day on the streets rudely healthy people seem to push us out of the way, thoughtlessly and effortlessly displaying a vitality and energy that has long since seeped from our muscles.

To know that someone else out there is also doing daily battle with a world of pills, waiting rooms, scans and blood tests, is limping gingerly between supermarket aisles and searching for the last seat at the bus stop, has had to give up the gym and the indoor tennis court or swimming pool and has learned the daytime television schedules backwards and sideways (which is how one often ends up watching daytime television – lying down) is a huge, if odd, encouragement, and I have been tremendously boosted by the letters of comfort and thanks from readers of several ages and all sexes. I'm only sorry I have been unable to reply to more of you.

So – terrors, panics and redundancies apart – what of the future? Well, I am buying every tombola ticket I can find for the great drug lottery. I am happy to become a lab rat for trials on the basis that my short time might as well be put to use, and could well suddenly become a slightly longer time if one or other of the treatments tested starts to work.

I am not planning for the future, which is hard sometimes to resist – thoughts of summer holidays in Lisbon, for example, have already started forming, but who can say where I will be at and in what shape by next June.

I am working hard – at home – enjoying the patience and generosity of an enlightened employer, writing reports on the future of entertainment media and wrestling with the early-to-middle stages of a second novel.

I seem to have plenty to do and plenty of people who want to do at least some of it with me. At times I feel that I am, for the first time, in full possession of my life: independent, at home, able to balance work, sleep, food and entertainment. Then, of course, something goes wrong and I am rudely reminded that I am no longer running my own body and have to obey the tyrannies of the virus.

There will be horrors ahead – apparently the CMV in my eyes will only respond to the current treatment for about six months – but, as Oscar Wilde said, 'Never put off to tomorrow what you can do the day after,' and, as Scarlett O'Hara added on the same theme, having inadvertently killed a couple of rebel soldiers, 'Oh, I'll think about that tomorrow.' So, for the moment I'm putting panic on hold and concentrating on the immediate: once I've done my shopping, finished my article, had my massage and read the paper, let's have dinner!

1995

4 February 1995

A monument of a man lost to loneliness

The taboo tattoo is beating its miserable drum again. The suburban sex police are patrolling our sitting rooms trying to shut down television screens and stop the neighbourhood watching such dangerous displays as lesbians kissing on Merseyside.

What is it with the British and sex? We are the nation that makes love with its eyes closed and the lights off and then, as it rushes to the bathroom for a gargle and a pee, yearns for sleep, pretending that nothing really happened and nothing more will happen for at least another month.

Maybe it's the appalling climate. Only those overheated by the inflammatory passions of love and lust can bear to go to bed bare, abandoning pyjamas and hot-water bottles for a bit of conjugal convection. Maybe it is just fear.

After all, the twin-backed beast of sex is an unruly animal that upsets the staid pace of suburban life.

For years, a po-faced man in round spectacles and a grey

gabardine marched the length of Oxford Street with a bill-board proclaiming that protein caused lust. Soon British researchers will discover that sex creates cholesterol, so we can all heave a sigh of relief, put our pyjamas back on and continue dieting into skinny celibacy, quelling the unsettling ebb and flow of tidal libido with sugar-free foods and high-fibre cereals as the focus of all conversation turns from the groin to the bowel.

The only problem is that the tabloids which attempt to dam(n) the sleaze supposedly oozing from our television screens are the same papers that make their livings peddling tales of Home Counties knicker-dropping, of sleeping around in dormitory towns and sex rings circling the suburbs. The current war on TV (television, not transvestite) sex may prove a dangerous boob in which the attackers become the attacked, the villains – the peddlers of outrage – become the victims.

How appropriate, when for the last ten years the same papers have made villains out of victims. In the catalogue of fatal diseases, Aids is the only one where the gay victim is found guilty until proved dead, while haemophiliacs are always described as 'innocent'. Perhaps it was this knowledge that led Leigh Bowery to such a lonely death.

I know I am not the first to offer up a tribute to Mr Bowery, but his death, both in its self-enforced solitude and its immaculate sense of timing (ringing the knell of 1994 on New Year's Eve) has a lingering poignancy.

Leigh was one of the monuments of our time – and I suppose if anyone wanted to argue that sex had a high cholesterol content they could have called on his monumental size as proof.

I was not a friend of his but I was an admirer. We met only twice – the first time more than ten years ago at a photographer's party. He looked magnificently daunting in a subtle and tasteful creation of multicoloured appliqué PVC and he regaled me with useful tips on how to seduce Australian policemen. Standing back, slightly in awe of this outsized diva, I began to wonder why it is that the testosterone-heavy culture of the Antipodes has created one of the world's raciest drag traditions, while the equally muscle-bound US gets very angry with cross-dressing. And Leigh stood at the apex of the world's gender-bending catwalk like the wayward son of that queen of the androgyne, Dame Edna.

Years later we met again, after a theatrical event in King's Cross in which Leigh, looking like a dimpled Russian dowager, miscarried on stage – both literally and figuratively – in a performance that might have been designed to appal had laughter not left the audience too helpless to build up any angry steam. We exchanged compliments – me about his show, him about my book – and smiles and I left, feeling as if I had just paid my respects to a postmodern Buddha.

Leigh could have had the world's most flamboyant exit, but instead the man who was at the forefront of Taboo – the Leicester Square club – became a victim of taboo – the culture of shame. The muse of Lucian Freud became the recluse of Middlesex Hospital. I don't blame him. I blame the others.

We have come a long way from the days of Donna Summer speaking of God's revenge but the Terence Higgins Trust still has to keep its doors locked against homophobic thugs and I still get letters from lonely, terrified teenagers, unable to tell their family that they are dying because they have not yet told them that they are gay.

So what are the white folk so afraid of? Maybe it's our fabulous sense of rhythm (have you ever seen a straight white man dance?). Maybe it's the fact that we can communicate with their girlfriends better than they can. Maybe it's just that they wish they hadn't slumped so soon into flab and gut, and had chosen Marky Mark instead of Mr Blobby as their fitness trainer.

Always acquisitive, gay men bought into body culture and acquired muscular superfluity long before immune deficiency. But I think the real issue is fear. There are many shades between black and white and the majority of men and women come in various tones of grey. Sex is the ultimate grey area. Many men, and, it seems, even more women, hover between poles, not always certain which way to turn and who to follow home.

Women deal with this well (in my experience). Men deal with this badly. I know many happily heterosexual women who engaged in equally happy lesbian affairs. But with men the lid is only taken off the Pandora's box of their mixed-up sexuality by the keys and levers of drugs and booze. Sadly, at the moment of greatest honesty, they are handicapped by greatest inability.

There are few experiences less enthralling than being mauled by a pissed hulk who is teetering towards the brink of his sexuality just before tottering to the floor.

I have obviously led a charmed life – I have never been queerbashed (it was normally my mouth not my dick that got me into trouble), my family has never turned its back or switched off its love, my boyfriend (who only had a year of fun before the nightmare started) has been a rock of support and a cuddly toy of affection when many would have said, 'Sorry, but I'm out of here,' and my only confrontations with prejudice have been on application forms for insurance policies. I just wish I could have lent that charm to Leigh Bowery (of course he would immediately have turned it into a bracelet) and he could have floated out of this world on the same magic pouffe of extravagance and invention that he floated through it on.

4 March 1995

Out of the driving seat, on to the bus

I ran for the bus yesterday. More to the point, having run for it, I caught it. This may seem small beer to you who commute, sandwiched between a few hundred bread-and-butter earners on a nine or five Tube. But for me the 'rush hour' had long since come to an oxymoronic standstill as, swept aside by the onward flow of brollies and macs, I was left beached at empty bus stops, washed up on empty platforms watching the back of a bus or Tube rush away from me. The problem was, I could not run. The neuropathy in my toes left them feeling as numb and brittle as icicles and left me off-balance and flat-footed, slapping my feet through pavement puddles like a panic-stricken duck (it is comforting to find that toes have a purpose, but disconcerting to discover that only after having lost their use). And no matter how hard my feet slapped (or stamped), my legs refused to respond to their urgent splats and splashes. Having turned to twigs in hospital, they now took on a seasonal bent and played dead.

There were small comforts to be chewed over (or gnashed at), even as the bus rolled away. Whichever clinic I was going to, there was no hurry; I didn't have to be anywhere afterwards and even if I was late and missed my place in the queue, I had time to wait. The whole balancing act between time available and errands runable had tilted. I had time in abundance. I was just a little short of things to do with it.

But times, and time, have changed. I can run for buses because my legs have grown from twigs to saplings and the frost in my toes has thawed. I need to run for buses because I have appointments for which I am already late. The pages of my diary are no longer retrospective (did I do anything today?), but anticipatory (have I really got to do all that tomorrow?). I feel well again. My weight, pulse, adrenalin and appetite are up. Now all I need is my T-cells to follow their lead.

Unfortunately, however, as I sank into the ancient tartan of a still more ancient double-decker, I heard its brakes grind to a slow halt and realized that in my eagerness to jump aboard a moving bus, I had chosen one that terminated at the next stop. And, being prone to metaphors, as others are to horoscopes, it struck me that the bus was a little like my life: I'm not sure if it is coming or going, if it will make the terminus or come to a premature stop.

These are exciting times. The papers are again full of new drugs and new theories. The T-cell, it appears, far from being casually decimated by an HIV awakened from the languor of a ten-year slumber by some internal alarm clock, instead fights tooth and nucleus in a war of attrition against the invading virus, and then, after years of bloody battle, collapses in exhaustion as an army of replicants conquers the corpuscles.

If the T-cells are no longer the helpless victims, but the brave defenders, then surely, with a little assistance, a resistance could be kept up against the occupying virus, until the allied forces of medical research and pharmaceutical innovation are ready to leap from the labs and, braving the bloodstream, overwhelm the vile viri.

Like families huddled round the wireless fifty years ago, I have devoured these dispatches from behind the medical front, and as suddenly as the year changed so did my mood.

In 1994 I acclimatized myself to a premature death. Resignedly retiring from life, I declined on my recliner, sinking to a low somewhere between despond and despair. I took comfort in small pleasures and narrow horizons.

But as 1995 starts in a flurry of breakthroughs, and ever cautious professors make radical professions of optimism, I am banking on life not life insurance. I have made down-payments on my future – a new cooker, a new suit, a new fax machine – and, having last year alarmed my financial advisers with the certain assertion that I had two years to live (I needed assurances that my insurances would pay my dues to my heirs), I now plague them with worries whether the same policies will reach maturity as I reach seniority.

But nothing is certain. The light at the end of the tunnel keeps going out of focus. My eyes are fading fast and the bitterest irony would be to be cured of Aids but left blinded by a herpes.

If the resistance is to be revived, it needs the smuggled armaments of trial drugs. T-cells can kill the CMV where the

Foscarnet and Ganciclovir daily drips can only confuse it. And already a crucial battle has been lost: I have relinquished my car.

It had to happen. I was unable to see, or even sense, anything approaching from behind my right side and was constantly (over)taken by surprise. Coping with the cut and thrust of the pavement was hard enough. But tripping over pedestrians is a lot less final than running over them.

Having lost my (visual) edge, I lost my nerve and all my lane-hopping, ego-revving dare-devilry slowed to a motorized plod. I plodded behind other people's tail lights like a short-sighted pug. I stayed in my lane. I never swerved. And when the floaters blurred my vision to an impenetrable fog, I prayed and kept going, arriving at my destination with a neck cramp like ice trickling down my spine. What was the point? But even with the cushions of Tube and bus passes and cheap taxi-cards, I was bruised by the experience.

Driving a car had come to seem inextricably intertwined with my independence as a citizen, my status as an adult and my potency as a man. So what if my supposed 2200cc virility was spent in pointless honking at stationary traffic? So what if my status was each year chipped away by a new generation of carefully redesigned models? At the very least my car was a telephone-free oasis. At best it was my de luxe portable Walkman. It's just that it carried me, not me it. No longer.

Of course, I know I have done the right thing, for the sake of children, other pedestrians, other drivers and the future of the planet. But when, last week, I came face to fender with my old car in the company car park (I was not 'visiting an old friend'; I was accepting a lift from a colleague), it was an emotional moment. There was so much I wanted to say. But I just knew it wouldn't understand.

Thankfully it was raining. But as I stood blinking in the dark, a voice called to me across the tarmac: 'Oscar, get a bloody move on. I've got to get home.' Things must be speeding up. I even have to run for my lifts these days.

1 April 1995

All there is to know about the crying game

Dear Ad, You're dead and I feel bad. I want to cry but I can't because the pain hasn't hurt yet. I want to cry but when C rang me from Sydney to tell me you were dead the tears flooded his voice and washed his words away and I just sat there on the end of the phone, the telly still on, dry-eyed, sensible, asking the right questions in an odd voice, and I felt like a piece of bone washed up on the sand and left to parch in the sun while everyone else frolicked in the waves.

I want to feel the tides of my tears close over your head and let you sink out of sight, but I can't. I want to hold your coffin at the top of the chute and pause to touch it before it slides into the sea, but I can't. You were already buried a week ago on the other side of the world. It has probably already rained on your grave.

I haven't dared stop and take out your pictures or read your old letters. I don't trust myself. I know I'll think I'm trying to trigger tears, trying to jump-start my emotions when I want them to rise, slowly, like water through a plant, from my guts up my spine into my mind out of my eyes and down my cheeks. I still need to clear a space. To spend some time alone with you.

But every day it is harder to remember.

You were already so far away it is hard to miss you more than I did. I suppose, after moving to Australia, there was only one move that could have made you less accessible, and now you've made it. It may be easier to get a visa to visit you, but they don't sell return tickets.

I was never very good at appropriate tears. I can command the full flow at moments of drunkenness, jealousy, humiliation and/or self-pity (a gang of four whose members are never far apart), but at times of profound grief I hold my waters like a deep pond.

I wasn't shocked by your death. Nor, of course, were you. I am still stunned by the stories of your strength in the face of weakness, your mental resilience to the physical debilitations of an illness that left you housebound and, eventually, chair-bound for most of last year. And I am sad that you never told me how bad things had got. But I know how hard it is to write and say how hard it has been. Especially when your sight is failing and your strength fading. Anyway, you always were terrible at self-pity. You always told me to quit moaning until I had something to moan about.

I remember the day you rang me, seven years ago, replying to a letter written in a state somewhere between hysteria and histrionics, in which I told you that I had been diagnosed HIV-positive.

'Get over it, girl,' you shouted down a bad phone line. 'I've been positive for two years.' Never have tears dried so fast. Never have I wanted them to flow again so much as I do today. But they won't. They never have. I didn't cry when Tim died. To be honest, I was relieved. He couldn't see. He couldn't hold his own cigarette. He could barely hold his own water. He knew I was there and he became flustered by my silence. But what can you say about your own life to someone on the brink of theirs? I didn't cry when Philip died either. I'd seen him shrivel into a brown husk, the taut dry skin stretched over his skeleton like a mummified body excavated from some desert tomb. I'd seen him in his wheelchair with an oxygen mask clamped to his face, his eyes rotating wildly.

I went to the loo and stared at my face and felt the dread creep up into my chest like frost, knowing that this could, maybe would, happen to me.

So, after C rang on that Saturday night two weeks ago, I went and sat in front of the television and watched the rest of *Platoon*, and I rolled a joint because I thought that was what you would have done.

So many memories have flashed into my head of you, in my rooms at university, calmly completing the joint that would collapse my planned afternoon of reading and unplanned dozing into another happy, wasted ramble to coffee bars through gardens via others' rooms, leaving a trail of abandoned books and disrupted study in our wake.

And as I sat there, I imagined you in the room with me and I wanted to ask if I should fly down for your memorial service and I could hear your reply.

'What's the point? I won't be there.' Maybe we should have

had a party. But it is hard to summon a festive phoenix from cremation ashes.

I went to one last week, arriving long after the champagne had been drunk and the vol-au-vents abandoned on cardboard plates. 'It will be a celebration,' I had been told by a close friend of the deceased. And as I suggested that maybe I wasn't a close or old enough friend to be there, she insisted. 'You know that N would want as many people as possible to come.' And I know that you would too, Ad, and that you'd want there to be unexpected seductions in strange bedrooms and too much drunk, eaten and otherwise consumed by too many too quickly.

We arrived at N's party swinging our champagne, in the mood for stepping out, but we were knocked back down the front steps by a mute huddle of friends clinging to each other in an amorphous mass of dishevelled clothes, their faces streaked with mascara. As they stumbled out, so we slid in.

People stood in corners clutching at empty plastic cups, whispering with friends, their faces drawn, their mouths pursed. We moved through the room unseen, invisible to guests immersed in their grief, blinded by tears, for whom an eight-hour wake was finally subsiding into intoxicating sleep.

And so, my wicked friend, the boy I depended on to lead me astray, the one who never said no and had never had enough, the soulmate with whom I never had sex, the cellmate with whom I was never vexed, the man with whom I laughed so often and lived so dangerously, I shall go to New York next week and I shall revisit our haunts and I will toast your ghost.

And I know that when this virus finally gets its teeth in my neck and shakes the life out of me, I shall be on my way back to see you. But, Ad, one thing – if you are going to meet me in a limo at arrivals, this time don't ask me to split the fare when we arrive at the club ... Oh, what the hell! You're bound to know the doorman so we'll be on the guest-list anyway.

29 April 1995

Just as the plot is getting interesting

One of my favourite snap-back witticisms of the Nineties was the chat-show retort of that bastion of wrongheaded rightism, William Buckley Jr., who described homosexuality as 'the sex that will not shut up'. I laughed and promptly stole his line. But I had to use it with care and only in certain company – preferably straight. After a few hundred years of secret indulgence in the love that dare not speak its name, gays had started screaming from the rooftops, dancing in the streets and nagging in the media.

I am not one of those who looks back longingly to the days of subterfuge and furtiveness, who longs for the hug of a straight (a.k.a. 'real') man and dreams of shadowy trysts in dark back alleys during wartime blackout.

But while the sentimentalized nostalgia for the eroticism of oppression left me cold and caustic, the new rabble-rousing of separatists and the professionally angry struck me as poison crushed from sour grapes. Maybe there should be a new noun, the 'tatchell': a creature who creates hysterical fantasies of vast conspiracies, a creature who, done down by the loathsome hypocrisies of society, seizes their weapons of smear and incrimination and runs up and down the country defrocking bishops. Surely, if we are going to engage in shock warfare, it should be in exposing the self-serving, self-repression of politicians, not looking up the cassocks of celibates whose entire – and happily largely redundant – institution has been founded on misogyny and homosexuality for two thousand years.

But then came Aids and everything changed. Hatreds and fears spilt out into the open, confrontations and repudiations spat bile on paper, on camera and on the street. And then, after the first paroxysms of fear and loathing were past, things changed. The shouting and screaming died down. The suffering was seeping into society. It was spreading its fear like tentacles into polite suburbia, strangling helpless infants, piercing the veins of haemophiliacs. Suddenly gays became vital ambassadors, emissaries, explainers and campaigners. Aids and our reaction to it transformed us from the pitied and the despised to the loved and admired.

But now the *Guardian*'s leading film critic tells us he is bored with our whingeing, and that a film (*Postcards from America*), made by a gay man (Steve MacLean) based on the writings of a gay man (David Wojnarowicz) who died of Aids, gets up his critical nose and, in his flip slap-down, is 'self-pitying'.

Never mind that this seems to represent a schizophrenia within the *Guardian*, which regularly publishes my whingeings on the disease theme. Never mind, either, that the film is far from preoccupied with Aids, but instead deals with the nightmares of child abuse and drug addiction, the desperate deprivations of runaways lost in urban hell and strung out desert landscapes, kidnapped, raped and beaten by lonely sadists in Winnebagos.

They just happen to be boys and their tormentors men.

And I should perhaps come clean and declare my position: I am a fan of Wojnarowicz, whose paintings and writings are the poetic regurgitations of a boy fed all the junk (food and drug and thought) that America routinely dredges into its diet. And I am a fan of this film. But my point is not to disagree with Derek Malcolm's critical assessment. He is paid for his opinions and will be until they are deemed irrelevant. But this gagging on self-pity reflects a sad trend: the falling off of interest in Aids just as the plot is getting interesting.

It seems bad strategy to abandon the film because the explosions have stopped, and miss the denouement when science conquers all. We've had the decimations and panics. We are now on the brink of launching a new armoury of drugs and treatments. Patients have reached beyond the medicine cabinet and found succour – even recovery – in blends of the traditional, alternative and ancient. I have not been this well in a year. I attribute my health, weight and energy to everything from acupuncture to prophylactics, from Chinese herbs and selenium supplements to ddC, septrin and Rifobutin.

It also seems bad theory to attack a film for self-pity when the entire US cinema of Vietnam is an elegiac exploration of just that. Never has a country felt so sorry for itself, as its public humiliation became private hell. Nor is my analogy far-fetched. Viruses are the new Vietcong, a guerrilla insurgent against whom conventional batteries of pharmaceuticals are helpless, and against which methods of infiltration and imitation become crucial. This is cell warfare along the Cold War model but fought in the jungle hot-zone of research labs.

But I am sure Mr Malcolm does not doubt the drama of the virus. The rapid success of Wolfgang Petersen's *Outbreak*, in which viral warfare translates straight from the lab test tube to the military helicopter in an *ER*-meets-*Die Hard* scenario, would prove him wrong and redundant. But even in *Outbreak* HIV has been demoted to a lower crisis category: the drama centres on a new fever, up there in the danger zone with Lassa, Hanta and Ebola fever.

What is depressing about Mr Malcolm's dismissal is the feeling that we had our moment of glorious tragedy and, now that we have become boring again, it is time for us to shut up. Unfortunately, I no longer find this suggestion funny.

Can you imagine Mr Malcolm berating a black film-maker for being boring by banging an old and much-beaten drum? A few years ago I wrote a send-up of Spike Lee, a small man with a large ego and a minor talent whose fury at the cluttering up of his platform with rival (and livelier) black directors had provoked him into some injudicious attacks on his compadres. (White liberal) tongues were instantly wagged in my face like fingers, (white liberal) *Time Out* – preferring a quick slogan to a serious debate – slimed me with the racist slur, while a gay black film director admitted to me in tired resignation that while he had a problem with my piece, he too had a problem with Mr Lee, whose virulent homophobia left him more chilled than stirred.

I crawled away from the row feeling suitably humbled. I

had badly misjudged the debate: to be smart-assed in the face of a few hundred years of oppression and denigration was to show a (white liberal) faith in an imaginary level playing field on which sacred cows had been left to graze in peace. There is no such field and the sacred cows stumble in and out of the media traffic.

But we have never made it even to that status. We are untouchable without being holy. Sex, it seems, will always be a stickier subject than race.

20 May 1995

The discreet charm of the pearl eyepatch

Accentuate the positive, accessorize the negative: this is my new spring season slogan. Having stumbled (those bloody platforms) out of Robert Altman's fashion extrav-organza *Prat at the Party*, I feel it is my duty to strike a pose-tive profile and wear my accoutrements with pride . . . and there are several of them. On a daily basis my pockets have to accommodate two large plastic bottles, each containing a balloon full of medication that gradually deflates and pushes either Foscarnet or Ganciclovir up a tube, through a needle and into my Hickman line.

So far so efficient: except that the tube from the Intermate device (developed by Nasa for astronaut food, so don't tell me I'm not hi-tech, cutting-edge or space-age) tangles with the wires of my Walkman, and the bottle gives my pocket a swollen bulge which I might use to effect if I had any libido left to exploit. But best of all is the Hickman line itself, which can bring Class 4B's swimming lesson at the Caledonian Road municipal baths to a changing room standstill.

Kids! Don'tcha love 'em? Don'tcha admire their natural curiosity and willingness to question? At Cally Pools, nobody batted an eyelid at the tube swinging from above my right nipple cluster . . . or at least not until after 2 p.m. every Wednesday, when Class 4B invades the changing rooms.

'What's that?' said curious, energetic and unapologetic kid 1, pointing at the tube. (It is about ten inches long and does lead even me to wonder if I have become an android and this is my power supply inlet.) Being a sensibly brought-up and well-educated liberal, I dispensed with obfuscation (mind your own business) or euphemism (I am a robot and this is where I plug in my battery pack) and went for the truth. After a sober but gentle explanation of my eye disease and the need to administer regular intravenous drugs, the boy looked thoughtful. For about ten seconds. Then he shrieked at his classmates: 'Look at this bloke. He's got a tube for his eyes going into . . .' With respect to Our Lord, I might paraphrase his wisdom: suffer the little children to stay in the schools-only changing room and not to come unto me until I have my shirt on.

But really, I'm not complaining about my new range of pumps, tubes, needles and valves. I have always had a penchant for paraphernalia. I just feel that the time is ripe for an entrepreneur with a sense of style to create a set of holsters, side-packs, front-loading flak jackets, syringe holders, stainless-steel needle packs and matt-black aluminium Thermoses for the litre and a half of mineral water I have to drink each day to stop the Foscarnet polluting my kidneys.

Notwithstanding my bashfulness in the face of the Bash Street Kids of Cally Pools, I know some will say I am simply seeking attention. And others will say I always have done.

There are probably still schoolfriends who remember my sudden sartorial blossoming with the arrival of punk rock in 1976 (well, 1977, really, but it's my history, I'll lie if I want to). I was not really a punk. I had no pierced body parts, hated cider and went to a 'posh' school.

And, to be honest, I found the music a little noisy. But punk gave me the perfect cover-up (or Cover-Stick) for a fashion paroxysm that mingled drag, kabuki, glam-rock and too much neat gin. There is nothing quite like the buzz of stepping into a crowded carriage on a Saturday night Tube and bringing every conversation to a halt.

I have sobered up since those days. My wardrobe is discreet. My hair is untinted. My eyes clean, if blurred. I am not seeking attention but I am getting it. And suddenly, as a return of energy has brought with it a resurgence of confidence, I don't see why I shouldn't enjoy it.

It started with the eyepatch. This is not an affectation. The oedema in my right eye shrinks, implodes and telescopes the world, warping people, buildings and cars into the crazed reflections of a fairground mirror.

Imploding heads may be amusing, but reading is hard work as my right eye superimposes a small and floating version of the newsprint page on top of the real-size one my left eye is quite happily reading. Given that my right retina has been so decimated by CMV that it delivers little more than a sense of perspective (the ability to reach for the salt and pepper without knocking over the flower display), I close it down with a black patch on Tube and bus journeys and during solitary lunches.

But necessity is the mother of pretension, and, while I travel London's transports in a discreet matt-black patch with scarcely visible satin polka dots, I do have a party range, courtesy of designer-decorator-domestic artist Shaun Clarkson. Shaun has bequeathed me part of a dismantled optician's display: a white pearl swirl and a green and pink sequin spin with beaded tears. For more practical business and daywear (as part of his *pret-à-porter* range) he is working on a Prince Edward check.

However, frivolity and facetiousness are close cousins and already I have had my new exuberance abused. Coming out to the opening of the London Gay and Lesbian Film Festival, I decided to don the pearl swirl. Unfortunately, my sartorial daring left me uneasy and off-balance. I had gone from victim chic to fashion victim and, moving through a cocktail crowd clutching a beer with a blind side and no sense of perspective, I felt off-balance and off-colour.

Eyepatches – probably like toupees – are hot and cumbersome, but once you've started it's hard to stop without exposing yourself . . . to ridicule, that is. I only sneaked mine off once the film started rolling, and after it had finished I fled under cover of darkness to find a taxi. But I was not going to get away so lightly. Out of the invisible space on my right side lurched the definitive train-spotter: unkempt frizz, unbuttoned duffel and overstuffed bag.

'You were wearing an eyepatch and now you're not,' he said in a revenge-of-the-nerd *cri de coeur*. 'What's the point?' I don't know what I should have done. I know what I did. I stuttered something about partial vision and eye disease and finished with a limp, 'And I really needed that,' which attempted to reverse the sympathy of gathering bystanders back in my direction. Then I plunged clumsily into a door that wouldn't open, turning my victory for pathos into a failure for farce.

I haven't worn the pearls or the sequins since. I've just got to get my nerve back. Attention seeking is not for the lily-livered. Now there's an idea for a motif.

10 June 1995

Turn the lights down low . . . please

My sunflowers are getting leggy, my nasturtiums are proliferating, my laburnum is in pendulous blossom and my cornflowers are in need of ruthless culling, but can I grow a beard? Can the Pope tango? The strange thing is, I can do the five o'clock shadow half an hour early and my three-day stubble looks like the charred cornfields of late summer or the bad make-up of a junior school Bill Sykes. But if I try any harder for any longer, these first aggressive shoots thin into spindly stalks guaranteed to leave my testosterone count in question and giving me the unwelcome demeanour of an underhand panhandler.

This is not the first time I have been let down by my body hair. This may sound churlish, but I never asked for a hairy chest. I was very happy with the smooth-skinned look. Then suddenly, in my mid-twenties, something (possibly a peroxide overdose) triggered the hair hormone and I went involuntarily primal. Not, you understand, the full shoulder, back and upper buttock variety. Just a dusting of the pectorals – but enough to conceal the curvature of contour I had invested three years' gym membership in cultivating.

I tried shaving – negotiating nipples with a Gillette and a prayer – and I dabbled in depilatories, trying to ignore the smell of burning rising from my scorched earth. But while for one night on the Fridge floor I could tear off my T-shirt and rip up a storm, by the next morning any amorous attentions from last night's lover could lead to a rude shock, as overnight stubble gave my chest the tactile attraction of a stinging nettle.

These days, my Saturday nights are more often spent defrosting my fridge, which seems unable to decide whether it is an icebox or an immersion heater.

Memories of bopping topless in Yvette's torso-to-go-go coolhouse are strictly in the cold store. So I have abandoned my creams, ceased fretting about the nips round my nipples and turned to face my face.

But only in the right light: overhead, dim and preferably indirect. I can spot an overlit, overexposed mirror at a hundred paces and will cross roads, eyes and dresses to avoid it.

Why all this fuss about facial fuzz? Can we talk – discreetly? Will this go no further? OK. It's my spots.

Don't laugh. We've all been through (z)it. Most of us emerged on the other side of the pubic wars and can look back on those days at the acme of acne as a battle that left scars more mental than physical. The rest grew beards.

I fought hard on that teenage front line, knowing that every new pimple would be the source of new classroom mockery as those who somehow got off spot-free (what did their mothers feed them?) zeroed in on the Monday-morning monstrosities nurtured by a weekend of bad cider, cheap sherry and No. 6 cigarettes. I waged war on my complexion with compounds and concoctions. I strafed and fire-bombed my face into a dermatological disaster zone. I scrubbed, chafed, scurfed and scraped. And finally, red raw and too tender to touch, I stumbled into the ambient glade of adulthood and rested. But not for long. Just when I thought it was safe to go back into the bathroom, it started again. Skin trouble.

It started with the itchy spots. Thankfully they began on my back, which, although hard to reach and scratch, was at least out of sight and, in quiet moments, out of mind. I developed a dependable technique for avoiding irritability during an irritant eruption: I sat still, closed my eyes and pretended that my back was being tickled, converting my raging urges (to scratch, to kill, to laugh wildly and run naked through birchwoods) into a meditative smirk known (to me) as the Zen giggle.

That was fine while my itching was undercover. But even the most placid mendicant would have been temperamentally challenged (or pissed off) when the spots broke out on his (my) head and neck. Flaming red and fiercely burning, they proved resistant to meditation, medicine and mediation (the forlorn attempt to talk them down), and only ceased their raging when I showed signs that I might cease living. As I plummeted into the fevers of septicaemia, they rose like rats to the occasion and fled this apparently sinking ship.

I survived and they, ashamed or just too alarmed, did not return. But by now KS had decided to get malicious and left a malignant footprint on my cheek.

Feeling less than radiant, I submitted to irradiation, aware that past therapy had killed the cancer but failed to erase its traces. To my astonishment, the blotch was botched and my face was in the clear (even if the rest of me looked like an overused blotter).

So what is my problem? Why the sudden renewed rush for (hair) cover? Well, it started in the gents' toilets on the third floor at work. I turned from the basin, where I was washing my hands, to the mirror on the wall just as the sun struck the side of my face and in a flash all was revealed: an army of molluscum was spreading from my neck to my chin and already advance parties had established expeditionary camps on my forehead. For those who don't know, these warty growths (is there any way to make warty sound less grotty?) proliferate laterally. That is, hit one and another five spring up in another place. It's like one of those kid's games ... except I play it every morning in the bathroom with a razor. Shaving, we call it at home.

Now, I know I have moaned about my molluscum before, and deplored the multiplication of my nipples, but, having just returned from Cannes, where appearances count second only to affluence, and the sun – like so many big stars – has a bad habit of shining too brightly on the wrong people, I have decided on decisive action. The only trouble is, I have not yet decided which decision would be most decisive, and, in the meantime, the molluscum have second-guessed me. As I dither over whether whiskers will give good cover – and, if so, whose I can borrow – the enterprising little growths have sprouted behind the hairline, leaving me scratching my head in a mixture of consternation and irritation. In fact, the ones on the back of my head have decided to stack themselves one on top of the other, so if you see me bemusedly and gingerly touching my scalp, it is not to check if my toupee is secure, but rather to discover whether my little 'friends' have broken cover and are winking at the world behind my back.

1 July 1995

A gut reaction to a bum kind of bumf

Mr Lucian Freud got it right. Writing in protest at my tribute to Mr Leigh Bowery some months ago he accused me of producing sanctimonious crap and suggested that to be 'posthumously shat on' was less than Leigh deserved.

Holy shit, I thought, as I carefully framed the signed postcard (of a woman blithely strangling a cat) and added it as a valuable asset in my will. How did he know? It's one thing to have a finger on the pulse, but he must have had an ear to my belly.

Advised against a war of words I succumbed instead to gut reactions. They are my speciality. Just hang around and listen in. I can give you stomach rumbles, high-pressure wind release and slow bubbling hiccups. I can add visual effects too, especially the wincing, doubled-up, red-faced contortion as I try to ease a recalcitrant air bubble through a spasm-struck diaphragm into my chest cavity and ultimately out into the open in an anticlimactic series of mini-belches and minor convulsions.

I sometimes feel that I may have developed a volcanic condition of Surtsee-style or Krakatoan proportions. Indeed, between that sentence and this I have had to take a fifteen-minute bed-break to quell a threatened oral eruption. Like most volcanoes, however, top-end solid eruptions are rare.

Gaseous emissions are, however, a constant tourist attraction and are often accompanied by lava seepage, known by its Latin description: diarrhoea.

I bring all this up (if you'll excuse the analogy), because recently people have been approaching me to test their products. Unfortunately these have not been six-week cruises to Bali, or government-approved daily doses of diamorphine (just to make me feel better). But they have involved my stomach.

Despite my chilly reception to their cold calling, the people in question went ahead and sent me their bumf by the bumper-load. This ran the gamut from shiny brochures with artfully shot pill spillages to photocopied medical treatises with polysyllabic titles written in a language closely related to – but ultimately bearing no meaningful comparisons with – English.

The vain issue was free radicals. This is not a mission to liberate political prisoners in the jails of oppressive regimes, but a plan to control the debilitating activity of certain destructive compounds through the use of antioxidants. Don't give up on me. I will go no further. I will not attempt to explain how judging the content of cholesterol in plasma was used to investigate the possible inhibitory effect of coenzyme Q10 supplementation on the cholesterol synthesis, or indeed what is precisely the antioxidative role of coenzyme Q10 in humans.

My response was immediate. I handed all the glossy brochures and the photocopied treatises to my doctor, I doubled my intake of vitamin C and I snuck into Superdrug and bought their own-label one-a-day selenium pills. To their credit, the company in question has never called me back. And, to be honest, I have a sympathy with the vitamin C plank of their philosophy. Ever since my mother put us all on a daily diet of fresh fruit, fresh juice and vitamin pills, I have survived every winter with a dry nose and itch-free throat. But I have the feeling part of the programme was that I should buy their products, and not just raid any old pharmacy.

However, while my vitamin C seems to keep me buoyant, even if its ascorbic acidity leaves me periodically acerbic, in general I think I make an unreliable guinea pig. Measuring the benefits of dietary supplements in a person who has an only fleeting relationship with food that seems intent on fleeing his stomach by the most easily available exit would seem a thankless task if not a messy business. Malabsorption is symptomatic in a system as malevolent as mine, and any medical tracts based on my digestive tracts would be at best maladroit.

But one thing has become clear to me since my days as an eight-stone shadow, hugging buildings to avoid the wind: food is good and good food is best. So while I am disinclined to plug the wares of my supplicant supplement salesmen, there is something I would like to share with you. It starts with smoked mackerel or spring vegetable and coriander pâté. It follows with a choice of stewed shin of beef with mushroom dumplings or aubergine gratin or Nigerian beef stew served with cabbage and courgette salad, and is rounded off with apple and orange pudding.

I would like to share this with you, but unfortunately it was only available in your home on Sunday 23 April. Every subsequent Sunday a completely different meal was on the menu, pre-prepared and delivered to the HIV-stricken by Food Chain, one of those services that restore your faith in man, and more importantly your appetite for food.

After six weeks of hospitalization last summer, suffering the indignities of five o'clock suppers (I have not eaten at five o'clock since I was five years old) my taste for food had dwindled to the occasional soup and a large glass of water and my weight had dwindled by nearly three stone. There is something terrifying about the listlessness induced by weightlessness. You never munch, you only nibble. You never finish what you started and sometimes barely start what you have cooked. Food becomes a burden and cooking becomes a chore. The occasional crisp seems to sate the equally occasional pangs of a hunger that is as elusive as an erection. And as you quietly starve, so you fade further into fatigue where the prospect of opening the fridge door is enough to leave you breathless.

Supplements may make sense (I still take garlic, ginger, multivitamins and Chinese herbs along with my vitamin C and my selenium) but not if they have nothing to supplement, and the core nutrition has to come from a daily diet.

That's easy to say, but sitting on the sofa in a sea-swell of queasiness, an Aero and a cup of coffee often seems like a three-course meal, even if it just produces a lot of hot air.

The hardest thing is to find the energy to make a meal that you want to eat.

My dustbin was filled with abandoned baked beans and

fizzy coleslaws. But the Sunday lunches delivered by Food Chain have the zest of the best restaurants. If I wasn't so heavy and relatively hearty I would be in the queue too. Instead, I'll have to buy my strawberry mousse off the shelf, *pret-à-manger* instead of haute cuisine.

29 July 1995

One giant leap for mankind

I thought I'd lost the knack. After thirty-five years of skilful manoeuvres, of great steps for man, albeit small backward paces for mankind, I couldn't pull it off any longer. Of course, a lot of it's down to confidence and a lot of confidence is down to youth. My greatest era was between the ages of nineteen and twenty-two. I made some spectacular wins with the sort of daring that comes from having nothing to lose (like pride, face, dignity, friends). As age accumulates fragilities of body and mind, as pride becomes tender and machismo tentative, sudden leaps of faith are harder to get the run-up to.

One look over your shoulder and you slap straight into trouble. Others are always quick to spot the quaver, then the mutiny is sudden and awful, the humiliation public and total, the loss of confidence utter and irrevocable.

I am, of course, talking about the ancient art of queue-jumping. There are those who at the mere words will turn away, muttering about morality and citizenship, about being

British and why we lost the empire. Fine. I'll see all you good sports and fine citizens inside . . . in a couple of hours, by which time we'll be cooking and you'll be steaming.

Of course, it is underhand and unfair, it is dishonourable and disreputable.

But it's fun and it works. For a few giddy moments you feel like the captain, standing on the bridge of the great one-upmanship of life. How can anyone be proud of such behaviour? How can anyone boast of such shame? Well, ladies and gentlemen, the shame is a sham, victory is the only vindication, winner takes all and loser lumps it. The more you seethe, the more we're soothed.

There is a certain challenge to be risen to. We are not talking matey mergers or gang clusters. The commando queue-jumper works alone and never looks back, down or nervous. He is a stranger to the guest-list but a 'friend' to the famous, knowing the best moment to fake attachment and latch on to the celebrity caravan. He is never recognized but seldom challenged.

And at the critical moment, facing an incredulous bouncer and remembering how badly you bounce, sheer nerve needs to be married to sharp thinking.

There are few line-ups more wound up than late-night clubbers and a badly timed jump can lead to a well-aimed drubbing and rather undignified blubbing.

My championship jump involved inserting myself and a 'close personal friend' at the head of an already irked queue of narked no-buddies. But our timing was off. As we slipped in front of three hundred bored teenagers, the door slammed in our faces and three hundred pairs of eyes bored into our backs.

Muttered challenges turned to shouts and cries, and I knew we had only seconds before we were torn apart, or worse still, turned back.

So, seizing the moment and the hand of my 'cpf', I knocked at the door and explained to the butt-faced mutt in the tux that I was part of one of the acts performing for the party and we were due on in less than ten. He fell for it and we fell in, leaving the mob to sob in our wake.

But there is a more dangerous game which makes Rollerball look like netball: the motorway three-lane diagonal ricochet, or how to get the wind up the wind-up who sits in the fast lane like a slug on lettuce. No flashing of lights, no bumping of bumpers, not a toot on the hooter required, just an acute sense of a wide angle. The idea is to spot a gaping gap in the slow lane and a couple of small spaces in the middle track, then calmly and without indicating (surprise secures the prize) you switch from fast lane to slow lane and back to fast lane in a calm, and dare I say, graceful, triangulation which leaves the road hog agog. If he then attempts to bump your bumper in a bull-headed charge, gently ease your foot off the accelerator and bring the offender suddenly nose-to-fender before hitting the gas and leaving him fuming in your exhaust.

As a former driver and ex-clubber, such smart moves are part of the past.

The nearest I get to zooming in on the inside track is a wheelchair ride through the airport (the perfect way to hop immigration and skip customs), but you do get stickied in looks of sympathy and the temptation to make a Lazarus-like leap at the last turn is hard to spurn.

These days, the whole magic and skill of the queue-high

jump has become at once bafflingly abstract and terribly concrete. How does one jump a queue that one cannot see, especially when, if you don't jump fast, you may not see at all? This is the riddle of 3TC.

Last December, I wrote about the findings reported in Glasgow on Glaxo's new wonder: a drug that in tests successfully inhibited the replication of the virus and allowed the immune system to regain strength. Soon after, I was told that it would be only a month before I could gain access to this success.

I was happy and content to wait. I knew that if the drug worked and my T-cells mustered strength they could save my sight and my skin (literally by reducing my molluscum and figuratively by increasing my defences). So I waited and kept a weather eye (left) open while wondering whether the other eye (right) would last.

Each month I was told that next month would be the month. My cell count was too low to qualify for the clinical trial, but I was up for the compassionate access. Next month came with no sight of the drug and less sight in my eye. I tried to remain calm. I knew my doctors were on my side.

Unfortunately, time wasn't and bureaucracy never has been. Paperwork clogged up and bogged down the access process, and seven months later I heard a whisper that all the drugs were being shipped out to the US instead of to us. I was speechless. My right eye was by now nearly sightless. The world had a habit of disappearing behind black blotches and now the future seemed to be disappearing into political botches. I had had enough of calm exteriors and good behaviour. I was feeling my way down the warpath. I bought a telephone microphone and prepared to ring a Glaxo honcho wearing the colours of an angry journo.

And then, just as my steam was building up a storm, my thunder was stolen.

My doctor called. The drugs had arrived. I could start on Friday. My karma had returned and I already felt calmer. My fight had been spoiled but my sight might be saved.

So, even as I write, I am twenty-four hours into the final count-up, watching to see whether my T-cells soar and let me see to watch my health restored. There's a light at the end of the tunnel-vision and I'm moving towards it.

Today's T-cell count: less than ten. Tomorrow's: watch this space.

19 August 1995

Floored by the urge to dance

My thighs ache and my clothes are soaked in sweat, my mouth is dry and my eyes red, my feet are blistered and I can scarcely walk across the room. I have never been happier. I have just spent four hours dancing to music I should have forgotten (but That is the way I like it, KC) on an impromptu dance floor with a calf-crippling incline, weaving between clumsy cousins and their ample if dishevelled girlfriends, nimbly outstepping lopsided aunts and loyal hosts, stopping only for a beer break, sitting in speechless, sweat-drenched transfixion, nibbling prawns and aiming conversations across a white-clothed table at the edge of the precipitous parquet.

For experts of the summer social whirl and its minor meringues, this will need no explanation. To others, less familiar with the archaic tribal ceremonies of the white folk, I have been doing the wedding weekend, and a much happier man it has made me.

Before you separatists start dipping your nibs in inky bile and blacklisting me as a covert collaborator, let two things be clear: I like weddings, I love dancing, and now weddings are the best – indeed only – chance I get.

Since having acquired an extraneous cluster of false nipples (a.k.a. molluscum), a ten-inch white plastic tube (a.k.a. Hickman line), a scattering of amoeba-shaped purple blotches (KS lesions) and lost all peripheral vision on the right-hand side, my willingness and ability to tackle the dark heart of the gay disco has vanished.

Now I know what it feels like to lose your religion. This was my temple and my pleasure dome, it was my exercise routine and my routine excess.

I was in there, ecstatic (more spiritual than chemical) in Heaven and Paradise, seeking out the hot zone of the Fridge and bartering my way into Trade. I was out there: grinning in intoxicated stupefaction, twirling my wet T-shirt over a wetter torso, flirting with whoever orbited my ambit.

Discos were my arena: I was the slave to the rhythm who tried prowling the fleshpit like a lion. Discos were my imaginary stage: dancing in my own closed little world, hemmed in by writhing semi-naked men (isn't everyone's private world like that?), I was the fastest quick-change drag act in history, switch-hitting as the hits switched from Patti Labelle to Mark Moore and any number of heavy petted shop boys.

Now discos are a danger zone. I slip and slide from off-balance to off-colour before being abandoned as off-limits. It has been hard, facing up to the prospect of a life without dancing, but when your balance is tenuous and your vision partial, your energy low and your confidence below the base-line, it takes more than a good bass-line to send you back out there, to get down as they pump it up.

I had to find my nerve and my feet, and given my neuropathy, the nerves in my feet. I knew it was possible after a New Year gift-trip to Jamaica found me spinning in graceful (or at least grateful) pirouettes as I soaked up the soca from a local sound system. But I was wrong-footed and unnerved by the prospect of braving a rave. They seemed so hard and fast, these ministries of dance. Like Nuremberg rallies where the beat battered you into submission, this was a crowd of the faceless getting witless while stomping to the humourless, leaving me helpless and, increasingly, legless. So I retired, adding dancing to the growing list of things we used to do when we were young . . . or at least fit and well.

I didn't like to talk about how I couldn't cycle any longer because all the traffic attacked on my blind side, or how I couldn't play tennis because the ball kept hitting my blind spot. I didn't dwell on my nights spent nodding off in front of the television. I tried not to flinch as friends described the night before on the morning after, trying instead to remember what I had been watching when my eyes closed and my mind switched off leaving the video switched on. I put on a brave face at their wild tales and resigned myself to the life of the prematurely retired.

I did my sit-ups and push-ups to calm my hang-ups about giving up and swam rigorous circuits to keep my currents vigorous. But dancing was a memory, sparkling through the fog of the past like a glitterball in dry ice.

Until this weekend and the wedding where it all came flooding back – the steps, the beat, the hits . . . well, yes, I have to admit, those hits. It is of course only at weddings, where the fashion police are off duty, that even the coolest customers get overheated to sounds of the Seventies. Beats punched like a bar code into the collective memory spin you back on to the tilted parquet like a zombie submitting to hypnosis. The good, the bad and the simply horrible leave you shaking and shimmying (a.k.a. staggering and wobbling) to music that seems to have been coiled inside your DNA spiral waiting to unravel. It would be unchic to mention names, it might Ring inappropriate Bells, suffice it to say we Got Down On It, Shaking it Down almost all the way To The Ground.

But the glorious truth I have rediscovered is that dancing is the perfect exercise and the perfect seltzer. So what if the next day you raise the roof trying to lift a leg into the bath? So what if your dance floor wiggle has become a hobble round the kitchen hob, or that your shoes, which last night were calfskin slippers, now seem lined with sandpaper bolted together with steel pins? The memory is still humming in your head like one of those omnibus *TOTP* reruns.

All that remains is the deletion of some unnecessary moments: like when you lost your footing and slipped on the train of the eldest bridesmaid and banged your head on her boyfriend's knee (even now that puzzles you . . . where did his knee come from?) before crashing into the candlelit peace of the table of hitherto blasé (now blazing) relatives. Like the moment when you and the drunkest of the drunken aunts became inextricably linked by her feather boa, glued together in a lipstick kiss and shot down by some bright spark's flashgun camera. Or the moment when, deciding against the rather tense queue of lip-chewing, knee-clenching guests hovering outside the loo you decided that the call of nature was the call of the wild and activated the garden floodlights while watering the flowerbed.

These are simply the hazards of an English country wedding and the certain sign that you have escaped the chill of your sickbed and a quiet convalescence on your sofa for the delirium of Saturday night fever. I'll take four weddings for a funeral any day.

23 September 1995

Positively positive

I bumped into a friend the other day in the waiting room for the eye clinic. I use the term figuratively. My eyes are stable and his are still good. I recognized him without a collision. But there is something about these occasional encounters in surgical anterooms that up the medical ante. Little time is wasted on social catch-up or superficial chatter. The normal how-are-yous of polite enquiry become the searching what-are-you-ons of medical research.

He had lost the pelmet of his vision, but the curtains had not yet been drawn and medical technology had advanced enough for him to take his medication (Ganciclovir) in pills and not the double daily doses (of Foscarnet) I still infuse through my tube. We exchanged symptoms and side effects, compared handicaps and compensations, and then I told him about 3TC.

Well, first I asked him if he had started on it . . . but he didn't know what I was talking about. So I asked him about

Rifobutin, and he looked blank (and blurred – the eye drops were working). Before I could explain, he was called in and I was left waiting for my pupils to widen, wondering why his knowledge was so narrow.

Of course I knew why. I have been there, too. There is something very tempting about opting for oblivion and lying down with the sleeping dogs to die. You are relieved of so many responsibilities. What can you be expected to do about global warming, the collapse of the pension base and failing standards in education, if you cannot expect to be alive more than twelve months ahead? You develop your own small version of the Bourbon retort. Grand, arrogant and slightly petulant, you repeat Louis XV's great historical raspberry: *après moi le déluge*. (Or given the current climatological drift, *après moi le desert*, and for those with a more religious bent, *après ça le dessert*.)

But it is a dangerous temptation, to switch off, give up, pass out and wait to pass on . . . because first of all you may just make it happen faster, and secondly it may not happen at all. My first response to the news of my 'conversion' (to HIV, not Buddhism – why is it that, in the PC vernacular of disease, the language of evangelism is deemed safer, or sounder, than that of sickness?), when a health counsellor asked me how I felt about being diagnosed positive and what I expected to do now, was meant to be sharp but sounded blunt: 'I shall go away for five years and live on an island in the sun until I die,' I declared.

'And what happens if you are still alive and well after five years?' she asked gently.

I winced. The plan didn't sound so dramatic without the

imminent doom lurking on its tropical horizon. Limping back to north London didn't really seem an option, and she didn't need to go too far into the health-care restrictions on your average palm atoll for me to clip my fantasy down to a much more suburban landscape.

But I got past my posing and now preach (quietly and only when asked) a programme of patient participation. It is a long time since ignorance has been able to guarantee bliss – the few I know who refuse to know live in a state of sweaty apprehension, in which every cough seems like a death rattle – but intervention can at least encourage prevention.

This is a peculiar condition affecting an oddball coalition and the gay part of this sad alliance has always been better at playing the consumer than the consumptive. The same skills applied to high-street shopping and shopping for street highs are now used to choose between a new set of brand names.

Already skilled in branches of the recreational pharmacopoeia, we have dug into the roots of more traditional botanica. Well practised in transatlantic traffic, we now traffick in transatlantic practice: if they are doing that over there when will we get this over here? We may not have the trappings of authority, but we know how to use the instruments of information and turn them into the powers of persuasion. And, while we have few political aides, Aids gave us medical allies: our searches mesh with their researches and suddenly an establishment so long protective of its exclusive expertise has become a partner in the investigations of alternatives.

There are risks: there have been false starts and culs-de-sac, blind alleys and (even) poisonous backwaters. But the great achievement of both sides – the patient and the doctor – is the dialogue between the treated and the treater, between the traditional and the alternative, the oriental and the occidental (and occasionally the accidental), the acute therapy and the therapeutic cure.

Of course, a little knowledge can be a dangerous thing. In the mid-Eighties, STD clinics were wary of testing any but the testiest clients. Without a cushion of counselling, or any apparatus of advice, doctors were terrified of the terror their diagnoses could induce. In a terrible reflex, some patients reacted to the news that they would die by killing themselves. It is a responsibility that still haunts the profession: how to deliver a verdict that does not become a sentence. But listening the other day to the story of a friend who needed her own melanoma diagnosis and wanted it over the phone, it occurred to me that we still had some way to go in learning when to tell the truth and when just to say no.

Fear of what someone will do out of fear is not a good enough excuse to keep them in the dark, and while many may baulk at delivering bad news down a phone line, judging by the way my friend's diagnosis was finally delivered the distance and detachment may have helped everyone. After a nurse had acknowledged that she had her biopsy results in front of her but could not divulge their contents, my friend waited two more tense days before going to the clinic to keep her appointment with the consultant. On going in, he asked her, apropos of nothing, 'Do you have children?', the sort of casual enquiry that develops sinister overtones in this context.

But when faced with the prospect of delivering the positive diagnosis and acknowledging the possibility that her life might not reach the end of the year, the man developed a stammer that left him unable to complete the word 'melanoma' . . . so he wrote it on a piece of paper and passed it across the desk.

With newsletters and factfiles, with help centres and information offices, the medical and the gay worlds have created a system that ignores hierarchies of knowledge. Access is the key, to your diagnosis, to your prognosis, and – crucially – as soon as possible to your antibiosis or prophylaxis.

Of course not all news is good. Today I read in one of the newsletters I subscribe to that the sparkle seems already to have dwindled around 3TC.

HIV is too shrewd to fool and has already found a way to mutate out of range. But reading, like writing, is something I can still do. And as the virus sits in my cells, reading off my genetic code and playing skittles with its sequences, the least I can do is try to catch up. I was never very good with my fists (fighting hurts, don't you know?) but give me words and feed me facts and I'll go down shouting . . . helpfully I hope.

27 September 1995

Aids: redrawing the battle lines

Oscar Moore, who entered the Delta trials disillusioned by the failure of past tests, reflects on the latest breakthrough in the long fight against HIV.

The girl from ITN said: 'We were popping champagne corks in the newsroom. It was so exciting!' She looked at me with an almost disdainful incredulity as I started pouring cold water on her bubbly. 'You've got to keep this all in perspective,' I said, knowingly. 'It's no good shouting too soon, because then when they do find the cure people will have already exhausted their euphoria. It's like crying wolf but the other way round.' She looked a little dismayed, even irked, but by then we had to move into my bedroom so they could film me injecting my Foscarnet, one of the two drugs I am currently using to combat the CMV (cytomegalovirus) chomping on my retina. And that, in a sense, is the key to it all – the fact that these days we are all doing two or even three drugs to fight one virus, and that the Delta trial results in all their statistical clarity have endorsed the whole principle of 'combination therapy'.

Viruses – and HIV in particular – are shrewd and awkward combatants.

Sometimes I begin to wonder if they are the inheritors of the world. Having lurked in relative dormancy for millions, possibly billions, of years, sudden changes in environment or in the habits of their hosts can lead them out into new territories, whether countries or host species. Hence the apparent jet-age theme of viruses breaking out of Central Africa and presenting themselves on the New York waterfront.

What makes these ageless antagonists so hard to grapple with is their ability to mutate. Throw them a curve ball and they learn to play curve balls. Throw them a fast spin and they (frighteningly) rapidly become adept at whacking them straight back to base. But throw them two balls from two different directions, at different speeds and at different parts of their body, and they go into a spin. They can't handle it. Yet.

This is the delight of yesterday's results, that suggest in broad statistical terms that the combination therapies of AZT and DDC, or AZT and DDI, hinder progression and cause a 38 per cent (in this trial) reduction in fatality. Not just that 38 per cent is a healthy number in a fight against a smart foe, but that the twin-ball throw works.

It is heartening for people like myself, who, having emerged from the disillusion of the long AZT-Concorde trial (whose final results offered no conclusive evidence of any measurable benefit from early AZT intervention), entered into Delta with a sense of resignation.

It might seem strange to applaud the results when the one group who didn't seem to benefit were those who, like myself, had already been using AZT (the Delta 2 arm of the trial), but a large part of this war is psychological: just as stress is a pernicious helpmate to the onset of illness, so optimism is a crucial part of defence. Mind and body are not separate, whatever five thousand years of religion has tried to tell us. The mind is, rather, a barometer and a valve, measuring and controlling the flows of the good-health enzymes that live hand in hand with the good-mood enzymes, even if that sounds cloyingly cute.

And, furthermore, these results endorse the theory behind other combination therapy programmes – whether it is the combination of Foscarnet and Ganciclovir I am throwing at the CMV, or the combination of AZT and 3TC I am using to fight, outwit and stifle HIV.

So while seekers of the sexy news headline may be sorely tempted to splash about words like 'cure' and wonder why they cannot and must not, this is a major battle won in a war against one of the smartest guerrilla insurgents around. Sometimes the military parallels seem astonishingly adept. I have sometimes talked of HIV as the grimly effective Vietcong facing the massed forces of the traditional medical army with its often redundant armoury. But the best analogy here may be much earlier – could DDC and DDI prove the Marshal Blücher to AZT's Wellington? Of course, I apologize to the French: but then the British regarded the swelling empire of Napoleon with as much foreboding as we now watch the growing domain of Aids.

What we have won is the fight for time. In the early years

of the disease, people died with frightening speed. PCP, a savage form of pneumonia, seemed to hit and kill within weeks. The problem was that people didn't know they were sick until they had a sickness. The lesson learned, slowly but surely, was find out your status, monitor your decline, and options will become available. The dialogue between out-patients' clinics and their patients was always straightforward: if we don't know (your status, your blood count, your viral load) we cannot help.

The great victory of the last few years has been the building of a sense of collaboration. No trial ever offers guarantees, but the happy results of Delta will bring a new energy to the patient–doctor partnerships that continue to play a key role in the development of treatments. And it will give many people a better chance to be alive for those treatments when (and if) they arrive.

21 October 1995

Autumn heaves

I have always looked up to trees (and down on shrubs). I have been a tree-spotter ever since, when I was five years old, my grandfather took me for walks by the Medway with the Observer *Book of Trees*. And they must hate this time of year. Just when it gets chilly, they're left standing naked in a field and expected to take a six-month nap.

Right now I feel strangely sympathetic. After a glorious summer in which I spread my arms, turned my face up and smiled at the sun, autumn hit me in the head with a pressure drop kick that has left me floored. As the clouds returned to the skies, messing up that wonderful blue backdrop, the trees started to shake and I started to tremble.

I should have guessed what was going on, having spent the initial eighteen years of my life with someone whose headaches were the best barometer of seasonal shift, short of the shipping forecast. But just as we believe our heads should rule our bodies, so we think that we alone can moderate our moods. So

I took to the sofa and waited for fever to reveal itself. It didn't. Nothing happened. It didn't even rain, and suddenly feeling high and dry, I threw off my malaise and flew off to Lisbon.

I won't recount my holiday (do drop by, however, for the picture-by-picture presentation of a hundred and fifty colour photographs). I will say that I felt happy, calm and somehow at home among the astonishing relics of a once-magnificent empire and a great nautical power. I think a Dutch–English ancestry is the best preparation for a Portuguese holiday.

But autumn was lying in wait. I arrived back in a London already wearing its long socks and unpacking its thermals, and immediately responded by running up the thermometer. It wasn't anything I ate. It wasn't anything I had drunk. It was just that particular skill of air-conditioning (in-flight or in-office) to leave the air in such a poor condition it functions better as a germ pool than a life source.

My head felt as if I was standing on it, my breath felt as if I had exhausted it and my legs had no feeling left, leaving my balance to chance and instinct. I tipped into the clinic and submitted to hours of tests for various members of the coccus family. I was cleared of meningitis and went home, already feeling better. (Sometimes all I need is a little attention, OK. Is that so bad?) I thought I had put this little post-holiday flight disorder behind me, and was ready to settle down to the main business of autumn – shopping for clothes you want but don't need – but no matter how fast I pushed off on the credit-card slalom, it was an uphill struggle. I couldn't shake off my shakiness, and by Monday morning I was quaking over my cornflakes.

This was not cereal-killer syndrome: this was the good, old-fashioned rigors. Up until now my shakes had been tremulous; now they were rigorous. I sat trying to read the paper and eat my breakfast, and ended up getting tearful over the spilt milk.

An hour before, I had connected my Foscarnet to the Hickman line in my chest, flushing an infection from the line into my bloodstream.

Having only recently wondered how things were back on the ward, with the sort of nostalgia that needs the confidence of distance, I was suddenly back in bed (number 6, Broderip Ward, right-hand side by the window), waiting for the food trolley to pick the least appropriate moment to come (while I was having my midday nap, or still reading the paper), trying to have discreet conversations with visitors when not eavesdropping on other people's.

I'm not one to make a drama out of a crisis, and apart from when I had the Hickman line removed with only local anaesthetic and no sedative (as discussions about why tugging at one end was not releasing the other got intense, I whispered something about not minding if someone wanted to put me out, so they did – out of their minds, that is) the week passed soporifically enough. I once again failed to read more than a tenth of the books and papers I had brought with me, failed to write one coherent line and slept through all the television programmes I had planned to watch. I was due to go home for the weekend and then return at 7 a.m. on Monday for the operation to put the line back in. But first I went to see my eye specialist. Except I couldn't. Well, I could see her. What I couldn't see, when I covered my left eye, was the eye chart.

Normally I can see a few of the big letters. Normally I can see where the chart is (it does, after all, have a light behind it).

Normally I can see the nurse, and when she says, 'Where are my hands?' I can tell her with a little more accuracy than the guess I hazarded: 'At the ends of your arms?' But not today.

This was Bad News, and a classic case of 'while the cat's away'. The infection in my tube had diverted my few remaining resources to a skirmish that left my retina unattended, and suddenly the virus, with its insouciant opportunism, had started to eat my sight again, getting through most of the remaining ten per cent of my right retina.

My specialist was to the point: we had to switch therapy fast – to a new drug, Cidofovir, which was on trial in the UK. Ah. On trial, but not at UCH.

At the Royal Free, at Moorfields, at Chelsea and Westminster . . . but not at UCH. And if I were to switch hospital, I'd probably have to ditch the Middlesex and take all my care elsewhere.

Was I expected to burn my bridges with the doctors and nurses who had cared for me, and not infrequently cured me, just because of protocol? I was cross, my specialist was cross, and we agreed to cross paths that afternoon.

I stomped off to Broadcasting House to talk to the people of Leicester about Aids and Pocahontas (I'm sorry, these are my specialities). I tried to look on the bright side but I couldn't see it. I tried to remain calm but I felt strapped into the back seat of an out-of-control vehicle. I was having what I believe is called a bad day.

By the time it turned into a good day I was almost too committed to fury to temper my temper, but as my doctor explained that the Royal Free would take me on its trial (patient 142 out of 150) and that I could still keep the doctors

I knew and cared for, it slowly dawned on me: no more Hickman line.

My new treatment involves three hours of intravenous infusion once a fortnight through a peripheral line, and so the thin white tube dangling from above my molluscum-infested nipples like some android's power-supply cable need not be replaced. My hi-tech stigmata, which I had expected to wear to my grave, was going. I felt like running topless through the West End howling with laughter.

Unfortunately, the doctors had other plans. Before I got too giggly, I should remember the sobering list of potential side effects from this new treatment: kidney damage, heart damage, low blood counts, low eye pressure, skin rashes, fever, nausea, vomiting, headache, shortness of breath and low blood pressure. Oh, but they forget. I am a veteran of too many trials to be intimidated by renal toxicity and potential carcinogens.

You know what really bugs me, though? When I left the hospital in the giddy blush of a bright new medical dawn, I forgot my pyjamas. My weekend was somehow completely unbalanced not by declining eyesight or by potential damage from untested drugs, but by the fact that my white-linen designer jim-jams had slipped into the hospital laundry and at this very moment were probably being steamed to shreds in a vat of industrial bleach.

It's the little things that get to you.

18 November 1995

Straight-talkin' gay

It seems a short journey out of the closet and onto the soapbox, judging by the brilliant – or at least dazzling – career of our latest Washington export-import (he left us for them and now has returned, briefly, to us as one of them). Plugging his new thesis, *Virtually Normal* (billed as an argument about homosexuality but sounding more like a soliloquy), Andrew Sullivan appears to have swapped the dog collars of the Anglican high church for the white collars of American high republicanism. But as religious faith has given way to political ambition, his evangelism appears to have acquired the smell of expediency. Not only has he made a vowel-movement to disguise his English origins, but he is also determined to keep his sexuality as battened down as his politics are buttoned down.

The assimilationist need that has him mimicking a passable Washington accent also finds him working to construct gay versions of heterosexual models (marriage, the family), while he takes conservative secateurs to the efflorescence of gay culture. Just as the born-again Christian outdoes the original in his zealous interpretation of ancient scriptures, so it appears the belatedly confessed gay seems eager to impose new strictures on his sexual colleagues.

If Dead Men Don't Wear Plaid, Real Men Must Look Staid. High camp is banned from Mr Sullivan's political boot camp. But, unfortunately, in squashing the hothouse (not always sauna) cultivations of gay subcultures, he may well be stamping on the grass roots of some of our most important victories.

This is not to say that Mr Sullivan has not made an important contribution to 'the cause'. In many ways, I like his book, although I am surprised at his need to pour cold water on new genetic evidence that suggests that nature, not nurture, plays the key role in matters of character, sexuality and psyche. Admittedly, this may raise the Mengelian spectre of genetic manipulation, but it at least repudiates the efforts of those determined to treat homosexuality as a sickness: the sexual 'doctors' who left behind them only the bitter residues of guilt and trauma, at best stranding their patients in a celibate paralysis, at worst driving their self-loathing to the brink of suicide.

Sullivan beats about the bushes on this point: unwilling to hitch his wagon to any dogma, he fudges, looking for a dead-end middle path in making the tentative and untenable suggestion that perhaps our sexuality is decided before the age of five ... or six. It is strange that he should cling to the anachronistic notions of strong mothers and weak fathers (and presumably not enough fresh air, vitamin C and regular football), when recent DNA discoveries seem to release us (and our supposedly delinquent parents) from centuries of moral blame. If our sexuality, like our hair or eye colour, is a factor of our genetic complement, then the moral fibre of the heterosexualist lobby turns to polemical porridge and we stand on similarly unassailable ground as those discriminated against for gender or race.

Sullivan teeters on an uneasy brink, perhaps too steeped in the rituals of his childhood religious refuge to abandon the cosy relationship with guilt that has fuelled fervid fervours for centuries. But I will leave him to examine his own demons – and their full genetic complement – at his own leisure. What is harder to swallow and difficult to digest is his broadside against camp.

On a recent edition of Radio 4's *Start the Week*, Sullivan attacked the portrayal of soldiers joking about cross-dressing in Molly Dineen's award-contending documentary series about the Prince of Wales' company, *In the Company of Men*. Sounding overheated and flustered, he blustered into a why-oh-why attack on gender-bending confusions that left his round-table colleagues in consternation. Why was this thought to be funny? he wanted to know. Why do people always camp it up when talking about gays? Hot under his white collar, Sullivan began to sound as ridiculous as a parade ground sergeant major. He reminded me of the small and angry man, vertically challenged and intent on challenging anyone vertical. But there was a sinister shudder to his anger. Some of the worst offenders in the history of aggression have been those burning a secret candle under their own obsessions.

I am not really suggesting that Mr Sullivan is attempting to wrench the drag out of queens. I do think he should study the politics of humour, however.

The Man Who Took Himself Too Seriously could join The Woman Of No Importance. And my point is not altogether Wilde of the mark. Humour has been the ammunition of our peacekeeping force and drag acts have been the crack troupes of our expeditionary (and exhibitionary) force. The men laughing over Julian Clary and Eddie Izzard may never have seen Lily Savage at her most feral, but these three men-without-agenders (sic) have done more to reduce, dissolve and subvert the old bulwarks of male bull than any informed testimonial.

Mr Sullivan would do well to watch Nigel Finch's movie *Stonewall.* The late BBC director's last film is an exhilarating dramatization of the landmark riot of Sixties Greenwich Village, and it makes a crucial point. As the grey suit-and-tie politicos go searching for the confrontation they need to spark the fire under their powder keg, they meet only the damp squibs of tolerance: they cannot get refused a drink, they cannot find the front line on which to start their offensive. Not, that is, until they end up in the Stonewall Bar, a haunt of the drag queens they find offensive and who find them tiresome troublemakers.

The truth is, living on the fringe of both your gender and the neighbourhood leaves you more prone to attack than banging on doors in the corridors of power, and our po-faced politicos suddenly find themselves caught up in a routine raid that accelerates into a riot.

It is a humbling moment for anyone who believes that debate between smart people in nice suits is the engine of change. And it is a slap in the face (from the man with slap on his face) to those who doubt the ability of the sexually subversive to undermine the morally aggressive. Without the courage of the Stonewall's frilliest and the routine brutalities of New York's finest, a riot would have been averted and a revolution would have stalled.

If you want to stand up and be counted, it helps to stand up and vaunt it.

If you want to get your message to the masses, it helps to make them laugh: the 'temporary anaesthesia of the heart' that led the best tragedians to intersperse their drama with comedy is an important precedent. Nothing is funnier than sex. It seems misguided to take the comedy out of sexuality.

Humour is our slip road on to Main Street. Our strongest weapons are not political grapeshot, but irony in the face of fire.

Mr Sullivan is excellent on the biblical bases (and lack of them) for centuries of proscription. He finds it harder to design a prescription for the future. His arguments are full of respectable quasi-family units, but we didn't create a flamboyant counter-culture to find ourselves co-opted into demographic condominiums. So before he writes off the queens and snorts at their plumage, he should be certain that his bile is not crushed from the sour grapes of an adolescence trapped behind the closet padlocks.

16 December 1995

Out of focus

Oh, shit! That was my first reaction as I tried to look wise, brave and cool, but instead looked appalled, crushed and confused. My second, as I got on the telephone to rally support for my wavering upper lip, was to collapse into tears in front of a room full of relative strangers and their strange relatives watching early-evening cartoons in stunned silence. Having poured my optic crisis down the fibre optic, I retreated into my corner cubby hole and, faced with the astonishing failure of hospital fridges to carry minibars, drowned my sorrows in the smothering comfort of clichés.

Behind every cliché lies an absolute, a wise friend once told me. Well, to protect you from every absolute (terror) there is always an appropriate cliché. I was just having a blind panic in the eye of the storm when, after all, every cloud has a range of available linings (including silver) and everyone knows that all's well that ends well. An operation (with as many stitches as necessary) in time could save nine lives and, at the end of the day, worse things happen at sea, don't they? Then I burst into tears again.

A plethora of platitudes can only provide a limited smoke-screen. That nagging voice always returns: So, what if . . . ? and, How do they know it won't . . . ? So, here I am now, writing this, ten tissues and a bag of monkey-nuts later (well, deep distress is like pregnancy, I guess – it does weird things to your appetite), struggling by the midnight oil (well, next to the early-evening Anglepoise) to make sense of this crisis, because after tomorrow I may not be able to see well enough to find the table without walking into it first. And, in my experience, a bruised face leads to a bruised ego which tends to shirk work and get shirty with the world.

Oh, shit! As Pauline Kael once said, I lost it at the movies. Watching an excellent new American film in the London Film Festival, I was completely absorbed in the sibling rivalries and amorous fumblings of *The Brothers McMullen*. So much so that I was keen to match real names to fictional roles when the end credits rolled. They came, and I waited for the screams of annoyance from the audience. But nobody seemed to have noticed that the names were so out of focus as to be completely illegible. I turned around looking for the man wearing three pairs of glasses who had cracked the code, and saw only rows of attentive people reading the screen. At least that's what I guessed they were doing. Their faces were a bit of a blur.

I had two choices – a dizzying spiral of inner despair as I faced up to the fact of my ocular erosion and faced down my peevish saline precipitations, or several Guinnesses at an Irish bar in St James's where the party started on the screen was carrying on in Sensurround. Sensibly deciding that crying in the cold wind of a November evening could only exacerbate the crisis, and that Guinness was surely able to reach the parts that even Heineken couldn't, I played the stout party and partied on stout.

O for such insouciance today. In fact, O for a few pints of such intoxicants. As I rushed out of the door this morning, already half an hour late for my appointment with the eye specialist, breakfast half-chewed and undigested, coat unbuttoned, Walkman unconnected, feet racing in one direction and mind in another, I didn't notice that I couldn't see. It had stopped bothering me that I couldn't see which bus was coming until either I was on it or it was on me. I had learned to lower my expectations and narrow my eyes and leave a certain amount to instinct. It was nothing to do with the blind following the blind. I was just going with the flow . . . and stop muttering about lemmings.

I thought it had something to do with November. November is a bad month for light. No amount of bonfires and fireworks can hide the fact that the sun has gone for a nap and left us with fog, drizzle, mist and gloom (they sound like the miserable cousins of the Phoenix family). The day is squeezed from both ends in the vicelike grip of a vice-filled (well, we can dream) night, and when the sun shines it's as encouraging as a warm gin and tonic with no ice and a wilted zest. At least by December we have learned to stay indoors.

And now, as December gets under way, that's where you'll find me, gingerly negotiating a flat that was once so familiar but now lurks like a fog-bound obstacle course.

You see, it wasn't just the weather. One glance at my left retina and my eye specialist was out of the door, looking for a second opinion. Why is it that second opinions always nod and tut, and then deepen your gloom by confirming the worst and ruling out the best? I must learn a technique for those moments of quiet solitude as the first opinion goes in search of the second.

Instant meditation, total introspection or maybe just rapid flight before I am left silently adjudicating their prognostications.

I didn't get away. In fact, I didn't move. I was experiencing one of the precursors to rigor mortis, diagnostic paralysis. So I heard those words: retinal detachment. Before you confuse this with visual irony or objective perspective, what this really means is a tear in the back of my eye. No wonder the tears are falling out of the front. The very thought is enough to make your eyes water. Of course, detached retinas are the day-to-day business of eye surgeons. For them, replacing the eye's vitreous matter is a simple solution involving simple solutions, and covering the tear with a silicon plaster is a technique easily learned with an inner tube and a puncture repair kit (different glue, of course – this one sticks).

The problem is that the problem is in my hitherto good eye. My right eye has been giving me little more than a peripheral rim of indeterminate colour since the Hickman line crisis, so I have been living by the left ever since.

I now face the prospect of three weeks of blurred vision on the left and no vision on the right (why does this sound like a state-of-the-nation address?). To be honest, I am terrified. I feel as if the abyss has decided to move into my flat. A world of talking books and plaintive phone calls looms out of the gloom.

But before I lapse into self-pity, I must remember the polite slap-down I received in the post from a mother whose son has to travel fifty miles for a routine consultation. It is easy for Londoners to develop that other eye blight, urban myopia, and forget that for those outside the charmed circle of the capital's teaching hospitals every treatment possibility involves the traumatic necessity of travel. It is enough to be unsettled by your malady without being uprooted by your therapy. Moorfields is ten minutes' walk from my front door. Sometimes Islington feels like downtown Med-City.

And then, of course, we can always look on the bright side (I'm just not sure with which eye): I will now be at liberty to get splashy with the face furniture. The solution may be simple, you see, but its refractions will fractionally differ from the diffusions of the traditional matter, which means that I can make a spectacle of myself with spectacles.

Georgio Armani? Paul Smith? Elton John? Liberace? Dorothy Parker for lunch and Michael Caine for brunch? Tortoiseshell or wire? Matt black or rimless tinted? I can feel a Christmas list coming on. Now where did I put my pen?

Why can I never find anything in this house? Has anyone seen my glasses?

Don't worry. Just practising.

1996

13 January 1996

Seeing is believing

I feel as Saul must have on becoming Paul. I want to spread the word and scatter the world with epistles on my epiphany. I can see again. I can read and write and even shop again. I can read sell-by dates in Sainsbury's and fabric contents in Selfridges. And, bristling with my new armoury of props and tools, I can even do battle with the West End.

To the outsider, this probably does not seem that remarkable. I had been told that the operation to reattach the retinal detachment in my (hitherto) good eye would take time to take effect, leaving me out of focus on the left and out of order on the right for up to six weeks. In fact, it has only been one month since I stood blinking on the brink of tears and fears, aware that all I could see today would be gone tomorrow.

The most valuable resource of the patient is patience. Convalescence and recuperation require rest and contemplation. But I can't get sedentary without sedation. It takes something momentous to damp my momentum. Finally, here it was: fog. Blur for me is more than just an overhyped pop hope: for the past month, it has been a whole way of seeing. As every headlamp refracted into coloured snowflakes, traffic became a haunting procession of suspended lanterns, luring this confused pedestrian towards collision. As every face was reduced to a pale pink disc with dark shadows for the eyes and hair, and a strangely shifting puddle for the mouth, I had to ask visitors, 'Excuse me, but who are you?' This I could handle. It was a cup of tea that did for me.

I had been all right until then. I came to after the operation in a confusion of pethidine, chocolate truffles and familiar voices. My parents had arrived (with the chocolates, not the painkillers) and for an hour I sat bandaged and blind, chortling with contentment as the opiates stroked my nerves and the truffles soothed my mouth.

Sated, doped and fatted, I slipped into sleep, and awoke the following morning in a disorientated daze. Stupid with sleep, I forgot I had a bandage over my seeing eye and fear rose like ice in my veins as I tried to make sense of a world that consisted of shades of grey. A nurse came and led me to the other end of the ward where the surgeon was waiting. As I sat there, silent with terror, he unwrapped my unthinking head and left me blinking in dazed and grinning confusion. Admittedly everything was a little fuzzy, but it was in colour and I could tell what were people and who were machines.

The operation had been a success, he said, and the lens was not cloudy, so cataracts – often an immediate post-operative problem – might not occur. My vision had gone from 6/6 to 6/12, which was to be expected and could be corrected with spectacles.

Bathed in the balm of good news, I ambled (gingerly) back to my room and ran a real bath. I was safe and happy and wallowing in the milk of human kindness (have you tried that bath oil?). Then, just as I was getting used to being waited on, a friend came to collect me. I hadn't really thought about anything beyond the immediate. It was a form of mental myopia: don't think further than you can see. But, muttering darkly and peering gloomily, I was shepherded into a cab and taken home.

Home – ha! A refuge, a sanctuary, a bolt-hole. Frankly, I bolted the hole as fast as I could. It wasn't so much the milling well-wishers whose faces I could not discern and whose concern I could not face. It was the fact that when someone brought me a pot of tea and a cup, I carefully poured the tea out on to the table next to the cup, scalding my legs and chilling my mind.

I felt stupid, desperate, alone and scared.

I wanted to scream and shout. I wanted peace and quiet. I wanted everyone to leave. I wanted everyone to stay. I wanted help. I didn't want to be crowded. There was only one answer: I rang Broderip Ward.

It was a Saturday morning. I had no referral. You're not supposed to be able to check yourself into hospital. It just doesn't work like that. But then, miraculously, it just did. Yes, there was a bed. Yes, I could have it. Yes, I could stay until I got a grip – or rather until my lover could come from the Continent to take me in his.

The world seemed a warm and cuddly place as I stepped back into the procession of Chinese lanterns and, with a friend to cling to, climbed into a taxi. I settled back into the seat and watched with contentment as the world, a strange and wonderful patchwork of colour, moved past the window. I was at peace. Seconds later, I was on the floor. The taxi had crashed into an unlit roadwork.

By now my self-pity had reached an existential level: I was clearly caught in a primal struggle between light and dark, good and evil, and I submitted to fate with a whimper and a pout. I pretty much kept up that pretty face throughout a week on the ward. Lost in the warm and cosy cocoon of a tiny field of vision – the size of one hospital bed – I emerged a week later, calm and collected (by my lover) ready to enter the world of optometrists.

I will never forget that first lens. When my specialist placed a careful combination of lenses over my eyes and suddenly her face sprang into precise, crisp detail, it was as if a caul had been peeled from my head. I was back in the world.

Since then I have grown impatient again. My glasses (two pairs on strings like the manageress of a haberdasher's, but minus the requisite bosom to rest them on) got tangled in my Walkman wires as I switched between near and far focus. I have wielded my white stick like a cattle prod, wishing for a mild electric charge. I have bleated when pushed, and snapped when stranded, and quietly tried to accommodate the terror of not being able to read or write without coming nose to page or screen with my book or machine. But last week something wonderful happened.

Having travelled up north to Christmas with my sister, I had forgotten my eye drops and was now on the train heading south, undilated and, I assumed, unfocused. For no apparent reason, I looked at my watch. Normally, of course, I just press the button and my special digital timepiece (courtesy of Islington Council) speaks the time in an electro-Disney warble that makes small children smile and parents frown. But this time I could read the right time with the wrong glasses. I looked around, hungrily searching for small print. I fished in my bag for books. I was amazed at what I saw. I was amazed that I could see. What for weeks had been an impenetrable alphabet soup now stood in orderly file and made words.

I have not stopped since. I read anything. I can read the paper (with a magnifying glass) while eating my cornflakes (with a spoon). And I can read my own grown-up watch instead of listening to the Mickey Mouse inside my speaking one (he still works the early morning shift when my eyes aren't even in let alone my glasses on).

But there is one thing I refuse to relinquish: my white stick. After all, how often does one get to play Moses in front of a sea of sale shoppers? And just imagine the impact at airport check-ins. The eyepatch already worked wonders on upgrades. With the white stick I could end up in the cockpit . . . all I need now is radar.

Oscar Moore was last seen heading for the West Indies from Heathrow airport. Efforts to restrain him were unsuccessful. He is expected back in April.

20 April 1996

Needle match

Isn't it always the way? Just after your birthday, after months of wondering what more you could possibly want, you suddenly realize what it is you need.

I am, of course, grateful to have had the birthday at all – time was (in late 1994) when I had decided I was unlikely to get through 1995, let alone reach 1996. I am grateful, too, for the stacks of CDs, some light listening (taped versions of *The Iliad* and *The Seven Pillars of Wisdom* – abridged, although I'm not sure if they cut the number of pillars or just made them all a little stumpier) and the piles of books (including a nostalgia-inducing *Encyclopedia of Vice* and, inevitably, two copies of the 'book of the moment' – John Lanchester's culinary voyage, *The Debt to Pleasure*).

So why am I grumbling, you ask, when I am clearly adrift among gifts? It's not that I am not pleased with the presents I did receive, but I worry that the books piled high on my bedroom side-table (including some unread gifts from birthdays thirty-five and thirty-four) will still be teetering over my bed as I stumble into oblivion. I'm not talking about shuffling off my mortal coil, but rather getting tromped by my miscreant *oeil*. The problem, you see, is that by the time I get round to reading them all, I may not be able to see them at all. There. I've said it. And this time I have remained dry-eyed. I didn't last time.

I thought I'd been doing pretty well, learning to respect my spectacles and return them to their receptacles so I could find them the next morning without too many obstacles. It wasn't always that easy. It has been an uphill struggle round a sharp learning curve. I have suffered the sickening sensations of a six-foot novice skier slipping backwards down the nursery slopes surrounded by agile toddlers doing backward slaloms, no hands. But my early pratfalls were not just humiliating, they were expensive. I had never imagined that wearing glasses required classes . . . so I learned my lesson the hard way.

Hard, as in the terracotta tiles of my bathroom floor on which I smashed my first pair of ultracool, suprachic, megapricey Air Titaniums less than twenty-four hours after collecting them, and having watched keenly (through the aspheric high-compression lenses) as my credit card lost all signs of life.

I had discovered one of the great conundrums of glasses: when you're not wearing them, you cannot find them. Not, that is, until you casually sweep them on to the floor and tread on the splinter of the self-same aspheric high-compression lens the optician has just spent three weeks hewing out of raw crystal.

For a breathless moment of speechless misery, I sat on the loo and stared at the out-of-focus wall, the glasses limp and cracked in my hand. I then adopted the strategy of repair that has always made my father wince and my conscience (a.k.a. my bank manager) twitch. I threw money at it. I had, after all, just thrown several hundred pounds at my face, so another hundred or so, just to make it stick, seemed like good money after more good money.

I have now learned about the relationship between glass, gravity, terracotta and bloody feet (as well as whimpering credit cards), but I am struggling with the tougher problem of day-to-day, minute-by-minute polishing, wiping, washing, spraying and wiping again. Featherlight and hypercool my glasses may be, but smudged and greasy they are, too, and I seem to spend half my life hunting out detergents for an early, late and mid-afternoon bath. I carry wet wipes, tissues, chamois and sheepskin. I have sprays in my pocket and spares (just in case) in my case.

But now I find that my hard-won facility with my designer accessory may be rendered irrelevant. Just as I am learning to live with (maybe even to love) my slimline, hypercool ultralights, and to amortize their cost – both intended and accidental – across every minute of every day that I wear them, I am faced with a blinder, literally.

I always know when my good eye is behaving badly because of the noises my specialists make as they peer through my pupil and make gestures to their pupils. On a recent visit, the noises were not good. Too many 'ums' and not enough 'aahs'. I flinched (but didn't blink), and then gritted and clenched as the noises were converted and the news was confirmed. The CMV was back – fluffy, happy and munching. I hadn't noticed any change myself, because it was still on the perimeter of the retina, but – I know those buts, they are a pain in the butt, no matter how wrapped up in ifs.

A day later, when my doctor asked me how I felt about losing my sight, I lost control: I opened my mouth, but the tears washed my words away and I was left feeling dumb and not a little damp. Things were worse a week later, and suddenly I was shooting up the medical fast-track again. Pulled from the Cidofovir trial, and its fortnightly, three-hour intravenous infusions, my next shot was to be not in the arm but straight in the eye. Fortnightly injections into the eyeball with my old friend Foscarnet – the drug that made me feel like a collapsed waterbed, but whose Domestos-style antiviral clout had managed to fight off all foreign bodies (apart from my partner) for a good year of crisis-free life.

I like it when doctors take control. When everything just happens too fast for you to think. I was still blinking back the anaesthetic, the iodine, the antibiotics and the dilating drops when the needle pricked and, seconds later, I was seeing stars and feeling like Jerry after he'd been whacked by Tom.

Gradually, very gradually, the Foscarnet diffused and the kaleidoscope settled. The world swam back into focus and the pain ... still didn't happen. Man, I was going to ring Bill Burroughs and tell him I'd done it, too (or had it done). What else could we try? People always told me acid in the eyeball was really cool.

So this could buy me a few more months and by then there might be new treatments and new options. To paraphrase a greater Oscar: never worry today about what you can worry about tomorrow. But I would like to be prepared for life at the end of this blind alley, and so far no one has managed to persuade me that life in the dark will be enlightening. Counsellors let me witter and doctors let me sniffle, but I want someone to turn around and say: Listen, Oscar, everything is going to be all right. Just put these on . . .

I am not being idle. I am doing the necessary research. I have been watching the current crop of sci-fi movies with more than a layman's laid-back gaze.

I am looking for technological options. Soft drugs are all very well, but I am ready for hardware. So if anyone is feeling bad about ignoring my birthday, here is my revised, postponed, but still operational birthday list: one ultragreen sensory headdress, as used by the villain in *The Silence of the Lambs* when Clarice Starling was darting round his dungeon; one cerebral videodisc implant to allow internal playback of other people's life-trembling experiences, as advertised in *Strange Days*; and one high-capacity brain-storage facility for up and downloading gigabytes of data (e.g. *The Iliad*), as featured in *Johnny Mnemonic*. All available at any branch of John Lewis . . . soon . . . please.

18 May 1996

Blind terror

Forgive me if I seem a little bruised, but I have just taken a rather sharp tumble. One minute I was Jayne Torvill pirouetting on thin ice. The next I was Tonya Harding crash-landing on black ice. I am still feeling concussed.

I knew my bolero was death-defying – all the evidence was against me – but there is something very disconcerting about hearing oneself dismissed as statistically dead. I was getting the message: I am past my cell-by date.

At a recent seminar on new treatments, one speaker blithely noted that everything he said applied only to people with a CD4 count of more than fifty, because people with lower cell counts than fifty had a life expectancy of only five to seven months. This was a matter of fact. Fatigue, shock and an uncertainty that if I stood up I wouldn't fall over prevented me from pointing out that, by his logic, I had been technically dead for eighteen months, having had a cell count of zero for the past two years. (Would anyone be interested in interviewing a member of the undead?) A week later, I asked my doctor how people coped when they lost their sight and what the norms were, only to find out that I had already failed to conform to the norms. Most CMV victims are gone before their sight goes, he observed.

I may have had a brief flush of pride at this point, but it felt more like heartburn. Then came the crash. I knew something was up as I travelled to Oxford for my injection. A bright spring morning was unaccountably smoky, like a suburban back garden in autumn, but without the comforting crackle of burning leaves. I decided to dismiss this as a bad-light day, sibling to a bad-hair day. And, anyway, every time I tried any sustained thought my mind was scattered by a sudden pain in my left temple, as if a gerbil had just taken a byte-sized bite out of my brain.

I should have understood the signs. There's no such thing as an innocent headache; no such thing as an insignificant blur (pop stars not included).

But I wasn't prepared to scare myself with the prosaic when I could blame the exotic. I had that perfect worldly excuse for being weary, having returned from New York only the previous day. The trouble was, I didn't want to think about that either. I had been shredded, minced, munched and regurgitated by New York, and felt chastened, weakened and wasted. It's not that I am a New York ingenue scared by tall buildings and big traffic. My New York track record runs back to 1979, and touches every rung of the social ladder from the Anvil to Studio. Got that? Yeah, sure, but try telling that to the Russian taxi-driver who still doesn't understand what you mean by 57th and Seventh until you write it down. Try telling that to the lady selling subway vouchers who just stares when you ask for a subway map (always a terrible moment of tourist confession). This is a city with no time to talk, no time for charm and no time for the weak. I guess it was an act of hubris (a.k.a. stupidity) to think that I could take Manhattan with one eye and a white stick. I had gone to write, to get away (like booking a holiday from the frying pan and choosing two weeks in the fire) but, like the white folk on the beach at Torremowhatsit, I overdid it on the first day. I went walkabout for ten hours and never recovered.

In Central Park, I was flattened by armies of rollerbladers (no sign of Larry Clark's Kids, otherwise maybe I could have just scored and gone home).

In Bloomingdale's, I was disdained by security for asking the way to the restroom (but found time for a nap in the disabled cubicle). And on Times Square, I finally lost the plot and went to pot (talk about smoking your way out of a hole).

I know what you are wondering: what is a partially sighted Englishman with a terminal condition doing in Times Square on a Saturday night after 9 p.m.?

Proving a point? Looking for a way out? Joining the Nation of Islam? Well, apart from the fact that my only distinguishing feature was being English, I was seeing a movie called *Flirting With Disaster*. And, given that the cinema was so dark I fell up the stairs, couldn't find the seats and accidentally sat in a wino's wet lap, the choice of film was pretty apt.

I didn't get much work done after that. I had overloaded my hard drive and suffered internal stack failure. In other words, I was too tired to think.

I reread the opening chapters of my long-gestating novel

and had a nap. I tried to figure out the toaster in my borrowed apartment and had another nap. The more I slept, the less I ate. I let one nap roll into another and then decided it was bedtime, anyway. Dwindling in weight and morale, I fled to out-of-town friends and spent two days sitting in a garden on Long Island recuperating . . . i.e., napping. So it should have been easy to blame my foggy vision and guerrilla headbangs on a combination of red-eye flight and nap overdose. Unfortunately not.

You see (I hate sight verbs!), the fog wasn't unseasonal bonfires or post-night-flight blur, and the headaches weren't random flares. We were at war, and losing it. The CMV had woken up with a hunger, and I now had so little retina left on the left that my vision was getting to be like US TV – hardly enough pixels to make a picture. I wish it was as simple as getting cabled. But this is not only bad; it is getting worse.

How much worse? You want to know? Four weeks left, which, by the time you read this, means two weeks to go. And then . . . curtains. As if to demonstrate quite how thick the curtains would be, I then had an injection of Ganciclovir that left me in profound dark and deep panic for half an hour. A sort of taster for future terrors, I suppose.

To be honest, I'm very scared. If anybody tells me anything more about occupational macramé, random pottery or abstract crochet, I will take them down with me. I have never even bought a National Trust tea towel. So helpful advice on self-help solutions gets a locked door and an angry-dog response.

But I have not given up. Tomorrow, I start a course of indinovir, a protease inhibitor (have you noticed how uninhibited my protease can be?). I have plunged further into the alternative pharmacopoeia and ordered a forty-five-day treatment of monolaurin. My injections have gone from fortnightly Foscarnet to twice weekly, alternating with Ganciclovir, and on the basis that everything is interconnected somehow, I am having reflexology in my feet to help my head.

In the meantime, I can't stop to talk. I have to see Seville, Marseille, St Petersburg (yes, I've done Naples, thank you, before you say you-know-what) and Damascus (and no, I am not trying to send up Saul). I have to read piles of books, watch videos of all the films I've missed and fill my memory banks with visual deposits for instant twenty-four-hour withdrawals.

But what about my career? I am, to put it simply, in the reading-and-writing business, and eyes have always been a tool of my trade. Well, I have an idea. If I just speak on to a tape, and then get some actor – someone low-key, like Sean Penn, say – to re-record my words, we could do cassettes of my column, stuck to the cover of the paper like one of those special perfume offers or giveaway Pacamacs.

How does Blind Man Talking sound? There could be an Oscar in it. Sorry!

15 June 1996

Realm of the Senses

When the going gets tough, the tough go shopping. That is my new, triumphant mantra. Not that I have become one of the vigilant(e) fashion queens doing boutique battle on the Bond Street front line. My appetite is more high-tech than haute couture, but I am feeling happier than the dowager who has just been squeezed into Versace Spandex, and I don't have to hold my breath all day.

Before you start warning me about crash-landings and post-euphoric despair, however, let me explain that I had started deep in the slough of despond (the fashion equivalent would be Slough High Street).

I had been getting quietly cocky. I had outlived the four-week death sentence passed on my sight five weeks earlier and, like John Major (as translated for us by Rory Bremner), I was muttering to myself with glee, not so much 'I'm still here' and 'It's still clear.'

My smile was suppressed and my joy cautious. I didn't want

to tempt fate. But beneath my sober demeanour lurked a smirk twitching to get out. Not for long. Remember all those schoolmasterly untruisms, like there's no such thing as gain without pain (while all around contented people made fortunes that only broadened their smiles)? Well, I'm sure there's one about the treatment being worse than the ailment, and if there isn't, let me coin it now.

OK, I am exaggerating. The twice-weekly injections in my eye were not that painful. But there was this danger factor: each time for up to half an hour after the injection, I lost all vision in my left eye, which amounted to losing all vision, as my right eye follows the left blindly, its retina destroyed by the insatiable chomping of the virus. Now, this was terrifying enough, and the relief of watching faces soak back into view inspired eager genuflections before the miracle of sight. But the terror became more intense when I was told that on any one occasion I might not get it back at all. It was a question of presure and blood. If the pressure in the eye stayed too high, the blood would not return; and neither, therefore, would my sight. This is called upping the ante and, at this point, maybe I should have quit the game. I ended up losing the round, anyway.

Last week's injections seemed to go smoothly enough, however. I didn't suffer a too-prolonged blackout and I left the hospital profoundly blurred but undeterred. Normal service will soon resume, I said, as we struggled off down Regent Street to the Royal National Institute for the Blind. Everything will become clear, I insisted, as we tried to understand the computer boffin supposedly demonstrating a talking-computer system but typing so fast that all the voice had time to do was belch half-completed words. All I need is to rest my eyes, I told myself, as I struggled around my room trying not to step on mysterious sharp objects. And then I slept and dreamt of trying to read eye charts with my eyes closed – because that's what they were telling me I had to do.

I woke up the next morning and was pleased. The sun was streaming into the room, and although everything was still a blur I had no doubt it would all fall into place as soon as I put on my glasses. So I put on my glasses and the only things that fell were my jaw, temperature and pulse. In other words, I froze.

The simple truth was that the injection had done more harm than good. The horrible truth was that I no longer seemed able to read. The immediate truth was that it was a bank-holiday weekend and the only responses to be had from all my clinics were answer-machines listing appointment hours. I always go into decline on bank-holiday weekends. They make me understand the principle behind the neutron bomb, which takes out all the people and leaves all the buildings. After pleading with a variety of answer-machines unlikely to be answered, I subsided into suspended panic and waited for the world to wake up again, or at least for it to get back from the beach.

Well, that's not quite true. I was mobilized by a team of concerned, intrepid and efficient friends. While one drove me to the optical boulevards of Wigmore Street, where we discovered a magnifying glass with a factor higher than two and a lens larger than a jeweller's eyepiece, another stepped up the hunt for talking books, computers and clocks.

I was as excited by their discoveries as I was exhausted by

my predicament and, newly enthused by un(fore)seen possibilities, snapped out of my paralysis and went to the cinema. It was just an experiment (involving Brad Pitt and Twelve Monkeys), which was like seeing the inverse of a silent movie. I could hear the dialogue but only dimly discern the action. So, while I was filling in the visual gaps with my own daydreams, I made a rapid decision: I was going to pull out of the injection treatment.

For some reason, I expected to be told off, or at least tut-tutted when I informed the pharmacy and the clinic, but my voice seemed to work like a mystical charm and one after the other, they said, 'Of course,' 'Fine.' Maybe they didn't believe anyone could stand two injections a week in the eye for long.

But more crucial than the medical implications were the consumer potentials. My friendly technofiend had unearthed a shopping trail heading for the Holy Grail of hardware . . . or Colindale, anyway, and a shop called Sensory Systems.

Now, the one thing that had really got my goat in all this ocular erosion was that I could no longer read. Of course, I could be read to – the list of books on tape was huge and ever swelling. But I also wanted to read the post, the paper and the large pile of books I had amassed over the past couple of years. My mother agreed to read to me once a week for two hours, but I needed fifty pages during the week and the same at weekends. Her redoubtable talents would be the icing on the cake, but how was I going to bake the cake itself? Well, to bend a metaphor until breaking point, I had just walked into the best baker in town.

Sensory Systems may sound like a technical department of the CIA but I am in love with its catalogue of hardware.

Indeed, as I sit here typing this and missing all the right keys (I never learned to touch-type), I am awaiting delivery of one of its magic boxes: the Aladdin Rainbow, which I am fully expecting to rescue me from gloom and return me to the glorious world of fiction.

Built like a computer monitor raised above a moveable plastic tray, the Aladdin has a camera in the base of the monitor that reads the text placed on the tray and then reproduces it on the screen. A lever on the right increases magnification, and a lever on the left allows you to change the colours of print and page. And I can lease it without any obligation to buy. After all, when your sight is fading as fast as mine, it seems silly to get splashy on the imminently invisible.

But then, of course, Sensory Systems isn't only for the eyes and the same showroom had a scanner that would read and reiterate an entire page of text. Of course, my mother is better – she is more mellifluous. But she is also less easy to keep on the bedroom table. I believe she's what you call high-maintenance. Compared with a computer, that is.

It's at times like these that I am prepared to worship at the altar of technology. Oh, excuse me. That's the doorbell. Now remember, Oscar, genuflect and pay respect (a.k.a. the deposit).

13 July 1996

Rub of the Green

I would like to stand and pay tribute to Trevor. Unfortunately Trevor has so rubbed me up the right way that I can hardly stand at all, let alone cheer his return from America. Trevor is my masseur. I shouldn't be so possessive about him, I know, but when you have felt Trevor's touch you will understand why I would like to have him move into my flat to be available at my whim and whimsy.

I should hasten to add that there is no monkey, funny, or naughty business to our relationship. Massage has been so tainted by the implausible euphemisms of the high street steam-and-rub joint that you can hardly raise the subject without raising a smirk at the same time. But the relationship between Trevor and me is strictly medical. This may cause the eyebrows of the sceptical to go vertical but even as Catherine Bennett's documentary series *Strange Days* pooh-poohs as voodoo every treatment that comes without a prescription, sceptics should get a new script. Sure, there are as many dodgy practices as there are shady practitioners and negligent patients. But to dismiss everything not readily available over the counter at Boots is to ignore the new wave of bionic biotics, mutants created by a combination of medical zeal and patient neglect.

But I come to praise Trevor. I used to be one of those who believed massage was just a slap and tickle short of frottage. Now, rather than just a nice way to unwind my mortal coil, I realize it is fundamental to keeping my coil wound tight and ready to spring.

After a year of accident-prone diarrhoea (and you don't want to hear about some of my worst slip-ups and let-downs) I was asked if I would like to have a more frequent – weekly instead of monthly – session at the Islington HIV clinic, and I leapt at the chance. Well, actually I went one further. I stripped down to my boxers and lay on the bed waiting for deliverance. I was ready, willing, and prepared to chant mantras and dance naked round reception if it would win me more sessions under Trevor's dexterous digits.

But while I knew that I would always feel better after a session, I never anticipated that I would also begin to look better and get stronger. By stimulating my erratic waste-disposal system the massage was regulating my flows and cleaning my flues. My skin shone and my bowels hummed. I could leave the house with a new spring to my stride. No longer the nervous clenching and the twitchy toilet-spotting.

But all that seems a long time ago. Since then I have become a full participant in the medicine of pricks, pinches, prods, and pummels. Monday is pricks – an hour of acupuncture, Thursday is prodding – an hour of reflexology, a sort of massage-acupuncture combo that treats the feet like a map of the body, and that leaves me Sunday for the Trevor two-hour special.

Everything was going swimmingly for a while and then I began to lose my sight and the government began to lose its vision. No matter how assiduously Trevor rubbed my eyes the view was still blurred. And no matter how hard Trevor and his Healing Circle colleagues stared at their bottom-heavy balance sheet the view was still grim. If they could not find new resources to replace dwindling council funds my prods and pummels would become a faint memory (my pricks were safe as I paid for them myself). Then, just as I seemed to be slipping towards a crisis, the abyss opened up and smiled at me, as if to lick its metaphorical lips.

I was simply walking down Liverpool Road on a sunny day rendered dull and murky by my fast-fading sight when the gardens on my right exploded into vivid colour. Like a child I moved towards them, attracted by their bright colours but also by the varieties of palm and tropical flowers that were growing through the railings, spilling their flowers onto the street.

But as I moved towards them they moved away. It was as if they were locked within the right-hand side of my eye and so when I moved my head to look at them they swung away and real grey world swung back into view.

I was not going to be put off. I had a lunch appointment to keep and no matter how many exotic hallucinations were thrown at me I was not going to be late. If two years of weekly LSD had taught me anything it was how to handle myself in public while hallucinating violently.

Unfortunately my lunch date was not so scrupulous in his

timing and I spent a strange ten minutes sitting alone in the restaurant fighting off encroaching visions. Sadly these were no longer the exotic botanica of the Liverpool Road. My new vision seemed more reminiscent of cheap wrapping paper than some imaginary Eden.

I managed to get through lunch without succumbing to the encroaching patterns, although my vision is now so poor that I did have to ask for my chicken to be chopped and my water to be poured. At least I managed to chew my own food.

But the real test was yet to come. I suppose in some way it was a near-religious experience, but at the same time it seemed more distracting than divine. The visions had calmed down a little during dessert and by the time we took our peppermint tea (so good for the erratic belly) I was even beginning to feel a little cocky. Unusual, yes, I know, but I blame it on the sorbet with vodka. As we headed back down Upper Street my companion kept grabbing my arm to prevent me from veering into the road and under the oncoming buses. Being a patient and friendly chap, I pushed him away irritably (clearly grateful that he had just saved my life). 'And who, by the way, is your friend?' I asked, pointing to the man on a bicycle who was cycling next to him at walking speed.

You can guess the rest. There was no mysterious cyclist at his shoulder. My visions were back, and I was a little pleased at their new religious overtones (OK, so the stranger on the road back into town from Gethsemane was not on a bicycle, but he might have been if they had been invented).

Things have got a bit quiet again now. My eyes have become so weak they don't even have the strength to hallucinate and I am typing this strictly by trial and multiple error (copies of the original text are available for demonstration purposes). But things are clearly getting a little precarious. So if you see a blank-eyed young man wandering the streets of Islington picking imaginary flowers and calling out the name of Trevor please put me in a taxi and send me away. It doesn't really matter where as I won't know the difference anyway. It's just good to know that even hell has flowers.

10 August 1996

Through the Looking-Glass

Would someone turn the lights back on, please? I can hear the splash and swish of car tyres on wet tarmac outside my window and I can hear rain rapping like fingernails on the glass, but I cannot see across the room, let alone ouside, into the street.

My horizons were already limited, and the loss of sunlight has left them like the T-shirts I inadvertently put through the hot wash last week: shrunken (well you try programming a washing machine that has a covered dial and a narrow red – i.e. invisible – programme selector with your eyes closed and see how your wardrobe survives! In fact, while you're at it why don't you try living my life instead of leaving it all to me? I need a break).

But there is a bright spot amid all this gathering gloom. I can still exercise my mind and hopefully exorcize my demons, by writing about them. And for this I have to thank the RNIB. I seem to have switched disability demographic in the last month, or at least gained a new classification to the AIDS diagnosis stamped on my life – like the CONTAMINATED label on all my medical paraphernalia.

As my eyesight has dwindled to only the haziest impressions of space and movement, a hitherto simple act like crossing the road has become an act at once of folly and defiance. (And will someone please tell all those well-intentioned roadside chaperones that it is uncomfortable, irritating and degrading to have one's elbow gripped in a crab-claw clench and be pulled across the road as if on roller-skates? At the risk of sounding churlish I would rather be left alone to figure out a way across than be manhandled like some wayward child. But then maybe I am foolishly clinging to an anachronistic desire for autonomy however illusory.)

I have entered the new (to me) and highly equipped world of the blind, a group more ancient, reputable (or at least less controversial) than gays, Tiresias' withered dugs notwithstanding.

AIDS departments may be on the medical fast track, but the RNIB represents charitable Main Street, with all the hardware stores to be found on any high road. In fact, I venture to suggest that this is the Bond Street of talkative tools and garrulous gadgets. At busy times my flat fairly hums with the chatter of talking watches, calculators, kitchen scales, bathroom scales (keep your voice down, please), and all manner of bleeping, whistling and ringing timers, detectors and measures (pity the poor burglar who decides to take a mid-break-in break and starts to make a cup of tea, only to be confronted by my ringing, singing kitchen.)

But, in addition to this chorus of chore-busters, this great and relatively ancient charity offers work-related retraining schemes. And so for two weeks last month I rose at six (Now don't get smart and suggest that everyone else already does. I am neither a farmer nor a commuter and prefer to take my cornflakes and boil my eggs at leisure, without having to first pump the cows, rob the hens or chew through a bacon butty on the run) and rode the rapids of London's rush-hour river, at least as far as London Bridge, where I joined the tiny rural contra-flow and headed out of town for the RNIB college at Redhill in Surrey. A quick tip for anyone with poor sight attempting to make the same journey – learn to count, at least up to five. Maybe I'm just dumber than most, but I failed to count the five stops from London Bridge to Redhill on my first day which left me wandering the platform at Horley, whimpering for assistance. Imagine my confusion and consternation when I discovered that it was now three stops on the next train back to Redhill – had I unwittingly fallen asleep? Had I passed through the British Rail looking-glass? Was I part of some complex spy-thriller? None of the above, I'm afraid. I was simply travelling back on the Victoria service, not the one heading for London Bridge.

Nevertheless, it was a severely discombobulated student who finally arrived for his first day of instruction, and one who was not comforted to learn that Redhill students were known for such involuntary diversions. I was not yet prepared to identify myself as a Redhill alumnus. I was taking a strictly Orwellian approach to the issue of identity: all men are handicapped but some are more handicapped than others. I felt like Jack Nicholson in *One Flew Over the Cuckoo's Nest*, a sense not helped by having found myself standing in a wedding-breakfast loo-queue behind Nurse Ratchett (a.k.a. Louise Fletcher) only a week earlier.

I have been in the real world, I told myself while dodging the muddy football being kicked somewhat erratically between five residents (yes, you could live here too, and judging by the disabilities of some of the inmates they had, too). I have travelled the world on transatlantic flights (tourist class, admittedly, but unaccompanied), I have chaired film industry conferences, and spoken on international platforms (at other conferences, not on railway stations), what was I now doing, feeling like a new boy at the wrong school, skulking among the bushes, dodging a muddy leather missile?

I was clearly having an attack of the rampant pomposities and, as if they had noticed, or at least anticipated, this reaction, the school authorities had designated as my guide and mentor a man who could have humbled the prophet with his ebullient display of cheerful resilience in the face of terrible adversity. Frank (not his real name) had run a sales and export office in a London factory for many years and recently he and his wife had decamped to the country, from where Frank commuted . . . until that is diabetes forced him into hospital to have both his legs amputated. As if this was not enough for one man to bear, whiled he was recovering the diabetes snatched away his vision, too. I began to get the message – even if I was not sure who was sending it. When I got home I listened to a television documentary about a blind piano tuner who had now lost his hearing as well. He could barely conceal his angry frustration at his new affliction, and I was humbled and appalled at my erstwhile snootiness. I sank into my studies like one seeking refuge from reality – a posture I had learned while observing my university tutors.

Whatever the qualities of the students, the teachers were a

marvel. Barring one, who tried to boss me around in the same way as she presumably did my less fortunate/rebellious colleagues, they were models of care, devotion and attention. Within seven days I had mastered the keyboard and was on my way.

I felt like a man dying of thirst who had been given not just a drink of water, but guaranteed access to the reservoir. Whatever the degradations and limitations forced upon me by my accelerating blindness, nothing would stop me from writing (now, don't balk).

So, with a talking computer to add to my chattering collection of knick-knacks, prepare yourselves for my latest oeuvre: *The Life and Tomes of Oscar Moore*.

This was the last 'PWA' Oscar Moore wrote. He died in Broderip Ward in the Middlesex Hospital on 12 September 1996.